The Way Forward

PLC AT WORK® AND THE BRIGHT FUTURE OF EDUCATION

ANTHONY MUHAMMAD

FOREWORD BY ROBERT EAKER

Solution Tree | Press

a division of
Solution Tree

555 North Morton Street
Bloomington, IN 47404
800.733.6786 (toll free) / 812.336.7700
FAX: 812.336.7790

email: info@SolutionTree.com
SolutionTree.com

Visit **go.SolutionTree.com/PLCbooks** to download the free reproducibles in this book.

Printed in the United States of America

Library of Congress Cataloging-in-Publication Data

Names: Muhammad, Anthony, author.
Title: The way forward : PLC at work and the bright future of education / Anthony Muhammad.
Description: Bloomington, IN : Solution Tree Press, 2024. | Includes bibliographical references and index.
Identifiers: LCCN 2023043620 (print) | LCCN 2023043621 (ebook) | ISBN 9781958590898 (paperback) | ISBN 9781958590904 (ebook)
Subjects: LCSH: School improvement programs--United States. | Professional learning communities--United States. | Educational change--United States.
Classification: LCC LB2822.82 .M849 2024 (print) | LCC LB2822.82 (ebook) | DDC 371.2/07--dc23/eng/20231024
LC record available at https://lccn.loc.gov/2023043620
LC ebook record available at https://lccn.loc.gov/2023043621

Solution Tree
Jeffrey C. Jones, CEO
Edmund M. Ackerman, President

Solution Tree Press
President and Publisher: Douglas M. Rife
Associate Publishers: Todd Brakke and Kendra Slayton
Editorial Director: Laurel Hecker
Art Director: Rian Anderson
Copy Chief: Jessi Finn
Senior Production Editor: Suzanne Kraszewski
Copyeditor: Jessi Finn
Text and Cover Designer: Julie Csizmadia
Acquisitions Editors: Carol Collins and Hilary Goff
Assistant Acquisitions Editor: Elijah Oates
Content Development Specialist: Amy Rubenstein
Associate Editor: Sarah Ludwig
Editorial Assistant: Anne Marie Watkins

Acknowledgments

To my family:

I would like to thank my wife, children, and family for your unconditional love for who I am beyond what I do. I strive each day to be better and to make you proud. I believe that I have a lot more books to write before I leave this earth, but you will always be my greatest contribution and legacy.

To Jeff Jones and Solution Tree:

You provided Richard DuFour and Robert Eaker the platform to spread the message of PLC at Work. A message does little good if it can't be delivered to those who need to hear it. You have provided so many outlets for schools to learn the PLC at Work process; the work could not have evolved without your support. I would like to thank every employee at every level for creating a multifaceted delivery model that makes it difficult for any educator to say they have never heard of the PLC process.

I would like to encourage you to keep advocating, expanding, and standing behind the message.

To my fellow PLC at Work associates:

I tried to honor your work in this book. The PLC process has come a long way since I was introduced to it in 2001. You have done so much to advance it. Keep pressing with a sense of urgency greater than we have ever had before. There are so many forces of darkness at work today, and you offer a ray of sunshine. Someone asked me how I feel about the current challenges in the field of education. My response was that it takes two combatants to battle; when there is only one side fighting, it's called *assault*. The sad reality is that many on the side of hope, inclusion, and optimism have stopped fighting and are victims of social assault. Courage looks like insanity to a coward. I am asking you to keep fighting and swing harder. Our field is at a critical juncture, and you are needed now more than ever. Choose not to tinker in the gray. Keep writing, keep speaking, keep coaching, and keep advocating for the PLC at Work process. We stand on the side of right and on the shoulders of giants.

To Rebecca DuFour:

You left us way too soon. We miss your great intelligence and your warm personality. Your contributions are highly respected, and we will fight to carry on your legacy, which is one of high scholarship, compassion, and a love for children and the field of education. I did not know Rick before he met you, but from all that I have been told, you made him a better person. So you not only gave us the gift of you, but also helped enrich the benefit we received from Rick.

To Dr. Robert Eaker:

Thank you for being a great mentor and gift to the field of education. You have been an anchor in this effort and continue to nurture protégés like myself. We appreciate your selfless service, and we will continue to drink from your fountain of knowledge for many years to come. You have been the embodiment of humility. You would often take less credit for your incredible contribution to this work so that others could shine. Don't think that high level of character goes unnoticed.

To Mike Mattos:

Thank you for being a brother and frontline soldier in this work of advancing the scholarship of the PLC at Work movement. You are a true testament to the power of collaboration. I look forward to many more years of thought leadership.

To Dr. Richard DuFour:

I wish that you were still here to read this book and give me all your unfiltered critiques. It is not easy walking in the steps of a giant. You taught me so much, and I pattern my steps after the legacy you left for all of us. Thank you for seeing my potential and pushing me to be the best version of myself. This book is for you and the unfinished business of making *PLC Right* the norm in schools. I hope I have captured your thoughts in a way that you would approve of. The fact that we are still grappling with your scholarship seven years after your physical departure proves that the body may leave this earth, but the powerful find everlasting life outside of their material existence.

Solution Tree Press would like to thank the following reviewers:

Shavon Jackson
Principal
Crawford Elementary
Russellville, Arkansas

Louis Lim
Principal
Bur Oak Secondary School
Markham, Ontario, Canada

Bo Ryan
Principal
Ana Grace Academy of the Arts
    Middle
Bloomfield, Connecticut

Jennifer Steele
Assistant Director, Athletics
    and Activities
Fort Smith Public Schools
Fort Smith, Arkansas

Steven Weber
Assistant Superintendent
Fayetteville Public Schools
Fayetteville, Arkansas

Bryn Williams
Principal
Leigh Elementary
Coquitlam, British Columbia,
    Canada

Visit **go.SolutionTree.com/PLCbooks** to download
the free reproducibles in this book.

Table of Contents

Reproducibles are in italics.

About the Author

Anthony Muhammad, PhD, is an author and international thought leader. He is considered one of the world's leading experts in the areas of school culture and Professional Learning Communities at Work®. He has been honored by the Global Gurus organization as one of the thirty most influential education thought leaders in the world in 2021, 2022, and 2023. Dr. Muhammad served as a middle school teacher and administrator for nearly twenty years, and he received several formal awards as both a teacher and an administrator.

As a researcher, Dr. Muhammad has published articles in several publications. He is the author of *Transforming School Culture: How to Overcome Staff Division* and *Overcoming the Achievement Gap Trap: Liberating Mindsets to Effect Change*. He is a coauthor of *Revisiting Professional Learning Communities at Work: Proven Insights for*

Sustained, Substantive School Improvement, Second Edition; *The Will to Lead, the Skill to Teach: Transforming Schools at Every Level*; and *Time for Change: Four Essential Skills for Transformational School and District Leaders*, and a contributor to *Beyond Conversations About Race: A Guide for Discussions With Students, Teachers, and Communities* and *The Collaborative Administrator: Working Together as a Professional Learning Community.*

To learn more about Dr. Muhammad's work, visit New Frontier 21 (www.newfrontier21 .com), or follow @newfrontier21 on X, formerly known as Twitter.

To book Anthony Muhammad for professional development, contact pd@ SolutionTree.com.

Foreword

BY ROBERT EAKER

Anthony Muhammad has written a book that is nothing short of a PLC at Work manifesto. Every reader will find the guidance they seek in these pages—from those who are interested in the PLC at Work process to those who are taking the first steps in implementation, to those who are well on their way to becoming a high-performing PLC at Work. *The Way Forward* provides educators at every level with a rationale and a road map for embedding PLC at Work processes and practices into both school and district structure and culture, and, importantly, Anthony sets the stage for why PLC at Work has the great potential to help educators face unparalleled modern-day challenges to provide schools and the educators within them with a path forward.

Context Before Action

The PLC at Work process is based on the assumption that people learn best by doing—but not by doing just anything. Effective change requires doing the right things—research-based, practitioner-proven practices—and having a deep understanding of the broader context in which organizational challenges and opportunities exist. A particularly effective aspect of *The Way Forward* is that Anthony outlines American education's history and education's present challenges to provide a context for the prospect of education's bright future through the implementation of PLC at Work processes and practices.

The Way Forward is also a rallying cry against what many refer to as "PLC Lite"—schools that have simply created a veneer of cosmetic structural changes that cover many of the same, mostly ineffective, practices that have defined schools for decades. The term *professional learning community* has become so popular it has lost any clear, common meaning. *The Way Forward* provides a detailed knowledge base that allows educators to avoid the PLC Lite pitfall and secure the bright future of American education that beckons us.

Beyond Convincing: A Call to Action

Recognizing that simply understanding, agreeing with, or even advocating for the PLC at Work process is inadequate, *The Way Forward* is an inspiring call to action that provides hope to those who want better schools for all children. Anthony makes us think, wonder, speculate, and, most importantly, question. Anthony dives deep into the why, the what, and the how of implementing PLC at Work processes and practices. He has written a common-sense, effective, and doable guidebook for those who choose to undertake or continue on the PLC at Work journey.

When I finished reading *The Way Forward*, I found myself paraphrasing Robert Kennedy: Some see traditional school practices that for decades have proven only marginally effective—or even harmful—and ask, "Why?" I see the proven practices of the PLC at Work process that, when implemented with fidelity and specificity, produce significant gains in student learning in schools of all sizes and socioeconomic backgrounds, both public and private, and I wonder, "Why not? Why not every school?" Anthony Muhammad's *The Way Forward* clearly demonstrates that we already know what we need to know to do just that!

Introduction

As a child, like many in my community in Flint, Michigan, I dreamed of becoming a professional athlete. In the 1970s and 1980s, Flint was a mecca for athletic talent. We had many role models to emulate, including professional football players like Carl Banks, Andre Rison, and Mark Ingram. Flint produced professional basketball players like Glen Rice, Roy Marble, and Latrell Sprewell. Flint is also the hometown of Major League Baseball All-Star pitcher Jim Abbott. My ambition of being an elite athlete ceased, however, when I stopped growing at 5 feet 9 inches tall and 145 pounds. I was still gifted enough to earn an athletic scholarship to Michigan State University, but my slight build and height ended my dreams of becoming a professional athlete.

College was not a bridge to a career as a professional athlete, but it was a means to gaining an education that would shape the trajectory of my life. I entered college with the aspiration of earning a degree in business and becoming a stockbroker. That vision came to an end after I sat through countless economics courses that could cure any case of insomnia. I transitioned from that aspiration to a vision of becoming an attorney, until I participated in a summer internship at a law firm, which revealed to me that practicing law in real life was not nearly as exciting as television shows like *Perry Mason* and *Law & Order*.

After these two disappointing experiences, I was a college student with no declared academic major and no direction. As I removed the factors of fame, fortune, and recognition, I found that at the core of my ambition was the desire to make a positive difference in the world. My experience as a student in the public school system had been less than memorable. I had earned good grades, but I did not remember learning anything I perceived as valuable or ever finding learning pleasurable. For me, school had been a chore, a means to an end. Fortunately, I had performed well enough to navigate that experience, but many of my peers had not. Like me, they had each grown up with the ambition to be a professional athlete; their genes had also let them down. Historically, those of us in that situation could depend on a secure job working in one of the many automobile plants operating in Flint in the 1970s and 1980s. As we departed from high school, those jobs started to disappear, victims of deindustrialization and global competition. The factories were automating, and companies were outsourcing, taking the only safety net that a dreamer could turn to once the dream died. I was lucky enough to get access to a university, but many of my friends were not as fortunate. The factories closed and the drugs, guns, and criminal underworld took their place.

A city that at one time was hailed as the lighthouse of American industrialization and prosperity was turning into a ghost town filled with blight, drugs, and despair. This reality led me to the conclusion that the only way I could truly make a positive impact on the world was to pursue a career in education and positively shape the minds of young people while they were still hopeful and impressionable. Education became my means of activism.

Shaping Young Minds

I graduated from college and became a certified secondary school teacher. I would later find out from an official at the Michigan Department of Education that I was one of only five Black male teachers in the entire state under the age of twenty-five. My first assignment was serving as a middle school social studies teacher in Lansing, Michigan. I asked the human resources director to place me in the school that had the most challenging student population, and he did. I served in this capacity for eight years, and I loved it. In 1995, I was named my school district's Teacher of the Year. I felt successful, my students enjoyed learning and felt loved, and life was grand!

Much as they push many good teachers, school district leaders kept pushing me to become an administrator, and despite repeatedly rejecting their offers, I eventually accepted and became a middle school assistant principal. I saw school from a totally different perspective in this new position. I became aware of the possibility of making a difference at a systemic level, and not just at a personal level. I thrived in this new position and eventually sought an opportunity to become a principal and lead my own school. My career had been personally fulfilling thus far because my vocation was directly connected to my moral purpose. There was one significant challenge, though: I possessed passion and sincerity, but I knew nothing about being an instructional leader and leading an entire school or system to greatness. It is safe to say that I possessed strong *will*, but lacked some essential professional *skill*. That reality would be disrupted and start to change for the positive in August 2001.

In July 2001, I accepted an offer to become principal at a school in metropolitan Detroit that was going through a rocky transition. I was hired to produce stability and move the school to new heights of performance. This was an ideal situation for me, but I lacked an understanding of exactly how to produce the stellar results my superintendent expected. That changed when I received an email from the superintendent demanding that all the principals in our school district attend an educational conference in Lincolnshire, Illinois—the Professional Learning Communities at Work® Institute. In hindsight, I was not pleased with this demand. I was a new principal, trying to get acclimated to a new environment experiencing tough challenges. The last thing I wanted to do was to take four days out of my schedule to attend a conference on a topic with which I was completely unfamiliar. But I traveled with colleagues to Illinois for an experience that would end up changing my professional life.

Connecting the Dots and Reaching New Heights

I attended the opening keynote session on day one with a pessimistic attitude, planning to sneak out of the auditorium the first chance I got. Richard DuFour, who would later become the greatest influence on my professional career, delivered the first keynote address. I was intrigued by his logical and articulate explanation of the Professional Learning Communities at Work (PLCs at Work) process. He was connecting all the dots for me. He was providing a pathway for my *moral* and *professional* purposes to connect. He explained that schools are places constructed to ensure learning success for all students and that the PLC at Work process is the best and most logical way to achieve this end. My skepticism turned into curiosity, and my curiosity grew into interest, and my interest morphed into fanaticism. I approached Rick and asked him to mentor me and help me bring this concept to light at my new school. During those four days, I became a PLC convert and zealot. I can say that I am even more committed to and zealous about these concepts today.

I returned to Michigan, and my staff and I dived into the process. We experienced record student achievement growth, an increase in teacher effectiveness and job satisfaction, and robust parental and community support. However, the journey was challenging, and it took us nearly three years to make a significant breakthrough. The struggle was excruciating at times, but the satisfaction of transforming the lives of children made the journey worthwhile. This school evolved to heights I never would have imagined before learning of the PLC at Work process. We were one of the early success stories of the PLC movement and emerged as one of the highest-achieving schools in the state of Michigan (DuFour, DuFour, Lopez, & Muhammad, 2006). I was invited to share some of our tangible successes and techniques with others at conferences and professional development experiences. People appeared to love the story and the documentation of the success that we were experiencing, but I noticed a reluctance among many to commit to the work and the change that facilitated that growth. This was very discouraging.

In 2007, Rick asked me to join the movement full-time and work directly with schools on the implementation of the PLC at Work process. I agreed to take on this challenge. This experience would allow me to scale up my positive influence from a systemic level to a national and international level. What became apparent early was that the commitment, vigor, and enthusiasm I experienced from my staff during our implementation process was rare among the schools I was assigned to support. In many cases, I found apathy and disengagement, and in some cases even malice toward the process. This challenge drove me to study and write about organizational change and school culture. These topics have dominated my research focus for fifteen years. The platform that I have been afforded has been a dream come true. My scholarship has allowed me to fulfill my vision of activism and make a difference in the lives of vulnerable children around the world through the positive transformation of their school cultures. Again, Rick DuFour's wisdom and foresight pushed me in the right direction.

In 2017, Richard DuFour, architect of the PLC at Work process and my personal friend and mentor, died after a three-year battle with lung cancer. In 2018, Rebecca DuFour, Rick's companion in life and in the advancement of the PLC at Work process, passed away too. These two events caused a major hole in the PLC at Work movement. How would we move forward? What was the future of the movement?

Facing Unparalleled Challenges

If those challenges weren't enough, the world slowed to a grinding halt in 2020 with the COVID-19 pandemic. Almost every rule of social engagement and normalcy was challenged, and the pandemic affected every aspect of human life, including school. In some communities, in-person schooling was replaced with virtual instruction for nearly two years. This abrupt disruption to school normalcy resulted in learning gaps for students of all ages and demographics. Both children and adults experienced unprecedented rates of anxiety and depression from social isolation. Teacher satisfaction and shortage problems, which began before the COVID-19 pandemic, became even more amplified. To add insult to injury, partisan politics started to use public schools as a forum to push political and social ideologies. As we look to the future, how do we overcome the mistakes and challenges of the past and intentionally carve a positive path forward? Is it time for those who heard the PLC at Work message in the past to take a second look? Could the remedy to many of our challenges have been hidden in plain sight since 1998?

Becoming the Architects of a Bright Future

I am concerned that our profession is losing its soul. In his book *SOUL! Fulfilling the Promise of Your Professional Life as a Teacher and Leader*, Timothy Kanold (2021) describes a person's *soul story* as "the pursuit of [their] moral good in order to create good in others" (p. 1). The weight of escalating political and social pressure to perform, never-ending innovations and disruptions to practice, low-wage growth, and public vilification of educators has led to an emotional and professional withdrawal that I have never witnessed within the scope of my career. We are at an important professional crossroads in education. We are in an era when simply knowing what needs to be done to improve our schools will not be enough. For nearly twenty-five years, educators have intellectually acknowledged the power of the PLC at Work process, but satisfaction with the status quo has been a barrier to universal implementation. The challenges we face today require us not only to acknowledge what our schools need, but to act on it.

When I attended the PLC at Work conference in 2001, I was not alone. Many heard the same message, but few acted. It is time for us to act with a sense of urgency because the future of our profession, our children, and our society depends on it. Time and circumstances dictate that we can no longer kick the proverbial PLC can down the road. We must all regroup, reassess, and do what is best for students. In this book, we will explore lessons from the past and critically analyze the challenges of the present so we can become the architects of a bright future for our students.

Turning the Page

This book is designed to be a journey. It is a comprehensive reflection of the past, the present, and our potential future. Each chapter represents a step in fulfilling the vision of high levels of learning for all students. Here, I provide a summary of each chapter of this book as a preview for our journey.

CHAPTER 1: A MOMENT OF CLARITY

Chapter 1 describes this unique time, post-pandemic, in which we currently find ourselves. I critically analyze the opportunity that the aftermath of COVID-19 has provided us—a moment that can shape our profession, our society, and the world for generations to come. The journey is not easy, but this window in time is uniquely positioned for substantive change, and the window will not remain open forever.

CHAPTER 2: THE PAST—HOW DID WE GET HERE?

Chapter 2 enlightens the reader about the educational challenges and movements of the past. We do not live in a vacuum; nearly every right and advantage we enjoy as educators exists because of the sacrifices of those who came before us. These advancements include the dismantling of racial, gender, and disability discrimination. What I have found is that most modern educators are unaware of the evolution of our profession, and many are apathetic in today's context. Activists of the past faced their own modern challenges, but they felt that their sacrifices in the present would lead to benefits in the future. Our system has not been perfect, but it has improved over the last three hundred years because people dared to challenge it and make it better. That same challenge faces the modern educator.

CHAPTER 3: THE PRESENT—WHERE ARE WE NOW?

Chapter 3 takes inspiration from chapter 2 and applies it to the challenges facing the modern educator. These challenges include teacher morale and retention, student trauma and mental health, inequitable funding and accountability systems, student academic achievement gaps, and political polarization about the roles of educators and public schools. These challenges are monumental, but I will make the argument that a full commitment to the PLC at Work process is the best solution to our modern educational problems.

CHAPTER 4: THE FUTURE—WHERE DO WE GO FROM HERE?

Chapter 4 helps the reader envision what our system might look like if there were a full commitment to the tenets of the PLC at Work process. This would include empowering teachers to agree on essential student learning outcomes, the proper use of common formative assessments, a multitiered system of student support based on evidence gathered through a valid formative assessment system, and extension opportunities for students who demonstrate proficiency on a particular learning outcome. We will examine the potential benefits for students, educators, and our community at large.

CHAPTER 5: STAYING THE COURSE—ARE WE ENGAGED IN PLC RIGHT OR PLC LITE?

Chapter 5 impresses upon the reader that full implementation of the PLC at Work process will require strategy and commitment. Simply reading a book or attending a conference will not be enough commitment to produce a high impact. This chapter will examine the roles of government, the central office, school leaders, and teachers in the strategic implementation of the PLC at Work process. This chapter will also provide examples of people who have successfully navigated this process as a blueprint for success and inspiration for those just starting the journey.

Meeting the Needs of All Children

This book explores a lot of the history of the public school movement, which is a unique movement in the annals of human history. Meeting the needs of all children is part of the foundation—the DNA—of the public school system, though we have never fully succeeded at reaching that goal. So a large part of my argument for fully embracing the PLC at Work process is to fulfill the promise of the public school system. I am aware there are private schools that are successfully implementing the PLC at Work process. This book does not intend to ignore your journey.

Private schools are organized differently than public schools. Though the processes of teaching and learning are similar no matter the format, private schools can select their students based on chosen criteria and teach the content they choose. Much of the public school history I cover in this book might not be historically relevant to you if you are a private school educator, but I hope that you find it morally relevant. Whether a student attends a local public school or a private school, the goal of ensuring high levels of learning for all students is equally relevant. Though private school educators may not feel the pressure and anxiety of standardized testing and public education policy, you have the same moral imperative to properly serve the children you are entrusted to educate.

Likewise, this book focuses on the history and challenges of the public school system in the United States. This is the country of my birth and the nation I know best. However, I have had the distinct honor to serve educators all over the planet. I have learned so much from observing and serving their institutions. Whatever your country, if you research the history of your nation's own public school journey, I think you will find some distinct similarities to the history I document. Though the dates and events may differ, the core principles associated with the struggle to produce an open and fair education system align. Our stories may be slightly different, but our objective is exactly the same: How do we produce a school system that is effective, fair, and equitable in its pursuit to properly educate our society's next generation of citizens? I believe that this book, and the body of literature associated with this book, can help any educator in any nation get better at this pursuit.

Calling for Action

This book is meant to be a call to action. Every chapter concludes with a format for reflection that I learned from Tim Brown, a fellow PLC associate and Solution Tree author. Tim encourages educators to reflect on their learning through three lenses: (1) Amen!, (2) Aha!, and (3) So What? *Amen!* is a metaphor (not in a religious context) symbolic of content that you agree with or that you find personally and professionally reaffirming—something that you've just learned that connects with your core as a person. *Aha!* represents content that is new to you—something that you found enlightening or view differently because of what you learned. *So What?* is a challenge and a call to action: "Now that I know better, what am I planning to do with what I now know?" After each chapter, I challenge you to process your learning and make it actionable. The process this book examines is called *PLC at Work*. If the content of this book does not move you to positively improve our work and our behavior, then I have not achieved my main objective. Each reflection activity includes a bee graphic because bees are some of nature's most productive, collaborative, and diligent creatures. Everything they do is for the greater good, and they fully commit to the process of collaboration. We can learn a lot from bees.

CHAPTER 1

A Moment of Clarity

The month of March in the year 2020 will always have a prominent place in my personal history. I recall listening to the prognosticators on cable news in the months prior as they predicted a cataclysmic and imminent global pandemic. The news reported a virus that shut down daily life in Wuhan, China, was heading to a country, town, and neighborhood near you. Personally, I was skeptical because I had heard this type of prediction before. We had been warned in the past about the apocalyptic dangers of swine flu, SARS, and Ebola, which were no more than contained regional phenomena.

I have been an educator since 1991, working both inside and outside of the school system. I have been a classroom teacher, an assistant principal, and a principal. Since 2006, I have been on the road speaking, coaching, and working directly with schools all over the world on organizational change and the school-improvement process. But my experience on March 13, 2020, made it clear that COVID-19 was *real* and *different*, and our lives would be forever changed.

I was in Los Angeles, California, preparing to fly back home to Detroit after conducting a leadership workshop. I stopped to eat at my favorite Los Angeles restaurant, Roscoe's Chicken & Waffles. As I waited for my food, everyone was fixated on the television news reporting that cities all over the United States were declaring "shelter in place" orders. I left the restaurant and proceeded to the Los Angeles International Airport, which was nearly empty. Upon arriving home, I learned that my home state of Michigan had ordered people to shelter in place. This triggered school closings and business closings, and life as we knew it grounded to an abrupt halt. Like most people, I found myself confined to my home with my family for months. Life had indeed changed drastically, and I was not prepared.

Tragedies and a Narrow Window for Innovation

Pandemics are interesting phenomena, and they are not new to humanity. The 1918 Spanish flu pandemic was even deadlier than COVID-19, and the disruptions to daily life were equally or more significant. As we prepare for this post-COVID reality, wouldn't it be wise to learn from the past so that we can plan for a brighter future?

In a 2021 article for the CNN website, Kristen Rogers writes that pandemics cause "a widespread sense that time has split into two—or pandemics creating a 'before' and 'after'—is an experience that's associated with many traumatic events." She points out that this feeling can actually give people permission to engage in critical changes to their lives and their societies that would not have been plausible under normal circumstances. She documents that the post–Spanish flu era brought about the following social improvements (Rogers, 2021).

- Improvement in personal hygiene and preventive disease behavior
- Advancement in medical research in the study of viruses
- Increased opportunities for women to enter the workforce due to labor shortages after the pandemic

So I think it is logical to ask, Are there improvements this post-pandemic window of time will give us the courage to implement? Should we look at post-pandemic life as a reset, or an opportunity to seize the moment for critical shifts in our profession? Issues like student achievement gaps, poor assessment practices, counterproductive public policies, and teacher preparation and retention were problematic long before

March 2020. I propose that, similar to the aftermath of the Spanish flu pandemic, we can take advantage of this transition from old to new to address some critical improvements to the field of education, and the PLC at Work process can serve as a pathway to a better future.

Critical Shifts and Commitment: PLC at Work Versus PLC Lite

The PLC at Work process, first introduced in 1998 by Richard DuFour and Robert Eaker, proposes that schools make student learning their focus, operate collaboratively, and take collective responsibility for student learning. Many educators have heard this message, but many have viewed it as a luxury as opposed to a necessity. The PLC at Work process has six critical tenets (DuFour & Eaker, 1998).

1.   Educators work collaboratively, instead of individually, and take collective responsibility for student learning.

2.   Educators agree to work on collaborative teams and engage in work that helps improve student learning.

3.   Educators clarify what's essential for every student to learn, unit by unit, regardless of the teacher students are assigned.

4.   Educators agree to administer frequent common formative assessments to gather evidence of student progress toward what the team has deemed essential.

5.   Educators agree to use the evidence gathered by their common formative assessments to provide extra time and support for students who are falling short of the target of proficiency, and arrange opportunities to extend learning for those students who have demonstrated proficiency.

6.   Educators agree to use evidence of student learning to guide their individual and collective practice.

Before COVID-19, many schools heard this message, but not nearly enough engaged deeply in the process. Though these practices make practical sense, the schools feared that, without a sense of urgency, educators would reject these critical shifts in practice because of the disruptive nature of change and a general sense of complacency. Many schools, pre-COVID, adopted elements of the PLC at Work process, but not an all-encompassing commitment to all the tenets. PLC implementation experts refer to partial commitment to the PLC at Work process as *PLC Lite*. PLC Lite best describes the current state of most professional learning communities around the country:

> Educators rename their traditional faculty or department meetings as PLC meetings, engage in book studies that result in no action, or devote collaborative time to topics that have no effect on student achievement—all in the name of the PLC process. (DuFour & Reeves, 2016, p. 69)

COVID-19 proved that we can make swift and substantive shifts to our practice when necessary. Many schools transitioned their traditional face-to-face instruction into a virtual platform in a matter of months. Teachers scaled down curriculum and focused on what was absolutely essential given their limited access to students and the collective trauma felt by both teachers and students. Educators found ways to connect and maintain some sense of social engagement, even though we could not be physically together. In short, we proved that when the situation was urgent, we could band together and change!

So why were we able to change critical educational systems in a relatively short period of time during the COVID-19 pandemic, but we made minuscule progress on critical improvements, like PLC at Work implementation, pre-pandemic? This question is worth examining as an accelerant to future professional ambitions. If we can act and change during a tragedy, we can act and change anytime we choose.

The content of this book is designed to be challenging, to cause some cognitive dissonance for the reader. I firmly believe that if we do not challenge ourselves and accept discomfort, improvement is nearly impossible. I want to affirm at the beginning of this book that I do not have a political, social, or ideological agenda; this book is meant for people of all walks of life. However, I do not shy away from any topic or ideology that impacts the goal of this book, which is *high levels of learning for all students*. In this book, I will address the policy platforms of both conservatives and progressives, Democrats and Republicans. I will address the history of systemic racism, sexism, xenophobia, and homophobia as it relates to undermining *high levels of learning for all students*. I am perfectly fine with disagreement with my theories and arguments concerning these topics. Disagreements can be powerful tools when sincere people are passionate about a powerful objective. Those disagreements can form a more universally beneficial compromise. I just ask that those who disagree put forward a valid argument with support for how that argument more positively impacts the education of *all* students. My guidelines for dealing with controversial material have three parts, and in this book, the content will stay true to the following guidelines.

1.   Is the content necessary and essential to the overall thesis of the book?

2.   Is the content true and verifiable?

3.   Did I present the content with a spirit of support, not malice?

If my content meets those criteria, I am satisfied and personally content with the reader's dissonance. Growth requires discomfort, and our tolerance for discomfort is directly connected to our capacity to improve.

Richard DuFour, one of the original architects of the PLC at Work process, valiantly fought lung cancer for nearly three years before passing away in 2017. He endured surgeries and treatments during his ordeal. He was often exhausted and in excruciating pain. Yet he continued to speak, travel, and write to advance the PLC at Work process. As the effects of the cancer disabled his body, he seriously started to think about legacy and succession. He pushed a few of his associates to support his wife Rebecca and his longtime friend Robert Eaker in advancing the PLC at Work journey on his behalf after his passing. During the last few months of his life, Rick would write me often. This led to many intimate conversations about his life, his legacy, and the future of the PLC at Work movement. In our most memorable conversation during that period, he laid a heavy burden on me, which I summarize here.

Anthony, I am going to ask you to do something for me. I have dedicated my entire life to advancing the PLC process, and my dedication has not had the influence I hoped. People don't disagree with the concepts, but most only implement the components that don't make them uncomfortable. I am leaning on you because I saw something in you very early: courage. You had the courage to approach me, a stranger, and challenge me. You carry yourself with confidence as an African American man with the surname Muhammad, and you are always authentic. I admire your courage. I am asking you to use that courage to boldly and unapologetically challenge people's misuse of the PLC at Work process. Make the message so clear that people would feel ashamed for not acting on such clear guidance. Tell

it like it is; don't worry about applause or people liking you. They can't cancel you because they didn't create you.

The emotion that gripped me at that moment was overwhelming. A man I had leaned on for most of my professional career was leaving. He was asking me to push the message forward in an unapologetic fashion. It took me years to fully reflect on and accept the challenge he placed on my shoulders. This book is an answer to that challenge. But I do not think it is fair to take on this challenge alone. I am seeking partners and allies in this mission.

I was interviewed for a podcast about my book (with my coauthor, Luis Cruz) *Time for Change* (Muhammad & Cruz, 2019). I do podcast interviews on a regular basis, but this one was especially memorable. After the podcast concluded, the host, my coauthor, and I engaged in a personal conversation for about ten minutes. The podcast host shared that he was concerned educators were not taking the dilemmas that face our profession seriously. He shared that he was disappointed with many in the research and thought-leader space because instead of sounding the alarm and being painfully honest, they were "tinkering in the gray." He used this term to articulate his observation of a lack of courage among leaders in this present crisis and how that lack of courage could have dire consequences. He expressed his appreciation for our courage to unapologetically take a stance on critical issues during the interview. This is what Rick DuFour was referring to in our conversation, and this podcaster's feedback validated his words for me.

The core purpose of the PLC at Work process is to achieve *high levels of learning for all students*. That use of *all* always excited me. I became an educator to address the needs of students typically left out of *all*. If this concept of deeply serving every student does not stimulate excitement at your core, then you can't be my ally in finishing the work Rick DuFour started.

- If you believe that some students have an inherent right to a better education than others, you can't be my ally in this work.

- If you believe that some students deserve representation of their history and culture in our curriculum while others deserve to be omitted, and laws should be weaponized to honor some and suppress others, you can't be my ally in this work.

- If you believe that the comforts of adults are more important than the needs of children, you can't be my ally in this work.

- If there are children in your school you deem disposable or acceptable casualties, you can't be my ally in this work.

The work of collaborating to meet the learning needs of all students through the PLC at Work process is often referred to as the *PLC journey*. Journeys are often long and challenging, and test every fiber of a person's being. This is why many people never complete their journeys. The PLC at Work journey is a journey worth taking and completing.

A Journey Worth Taking

The Alchemist (Coelho, 1993) is an epic tale of the journey of a Spanish shepherd boy named Santiago. Santiago has a recurring dream of a treasure awaiting him at the pyramids of Egypt. He has no idea how to get to the pyramids, nor does he know exactly where his treasure is buried, but his vision is so compelling that it is worth pursuing. So Santiago sells his sheep and takes a turbulent journey to Egypt to find his treasure. Along the way, he has many challenges, some even life-threatening. The temptation to give up and return to the life he knew before is common as Santiago confronts and conquers one challenge after another. Along his journey, he is robbed, beaten, and nearly killed. He also experiences some triumphs that are almost seductive enough to make him stop short of his ultimate goal. Through many trials and challenges, Santiago arrives at the pyramids only to find that his treasure is buried at a spot back in Spain where he would sleep almost every night. He had to go through a painful journey just to find out the treasure has been beneath his feet the entire time. Santiago returns to Spain, digs up the treasure, and finds it is greater than he could have ever imagined.

We have been through quite a journey as a profession and as professionals, from the conception of public schooling to the present day of its history. This journey is a noble one. The goal has always been to create an institution that invests in the holistic development of human beings with the intent of improving individual liberty and social vibrance. John Dewey (1939) connects the reality of schooling with the idealism of the American concept formulated by Thomas Jefferson:

> The right to pursue happiness stood with Jefferson for nothing less than the claim of every human being to choose his own career and to act upon his own choice and judgment free from restraints and constraints imposed by the arbitrary will of other human beings. (p. 161)

Like Santiago, we are on a journey that will yield treasures beyond our wildest dreams. Instead of rubies and gold, we have an opportunity to shape the future and unleash the positive impact of human potential on the entire planet. There have been and will continue to be painful bumps in the road. Some challenges are so painful that we might even consider giving up or settling for something less than the goal. I implore us not to settle or give up, but to work together and persevere; absorb the pain and learn the lessons. At the end of this journey, like Santiago, we will realize that the treasure has always been buried at our feet, but the lessons learned in our journey will allow us to appreciate and cherish that treasure. That treasure is student learning, and the tool to access that treasure is the PLC at Work process.

The Way Forward

Now that pandemic restrictions have eased and we have settled into this new normal, will we go back to our old habits, or will we take advantage of this spirit of critical change and action? I hope that we choose the latter. As Rogers (2021) points out, pandemics and social tragedies provide us with only a short window of time to make substantive change. I would like to propose a wish list of four critical changes to consider that would transform our profession for years to come.

1. Commit to truly working collaboratively, and build the infrastructure to support true teacher collaboration and professional engagement. This would include setting aside at least an hour per week solely dedicated to teacher collaboration and professional growth.

2. Stop focusing on achieving acceptable test scores simply to get a favorable rating by the state department of education, and instead focus intensely on making sure that each student masters the small set of absolutely essential learning outcomes in every course and every unit of instruction. Commit to using assessments to gather critical evidence of student learning and building systems of support that act with a sense of urgency when student needs are identified. When we stop focusing on external recognition and truly work together to relentlessly pursue deep learning for every student, our culture improves.

3. Unify to put pressure on state and federal lawmakers to pay teachers a living wage and to relieve schools from the tyranny of test-based rewards and punishments. During the pandemic, most states waived their state testing requirements to allow schools to focus on simply serving students.

They did this because it was humane and it was the right thing to do. Post-pandemic, it is still humane and the right thing to do.

4. Improve the ethics of our professional conduct and create an environment where intellectualism can thrive. Speak up when a colleague demeans a student or a parent or behaves in a way that stains and embarrasses our profession. We cannot expect others to respect the profession if we don't behave like professionals.

We are entering an era of renewal and opportunity. Let's not simply settle for the old normal; let's create a new normal—a reality where we can build a foundation for future generations of educators and students. And one hundred years from now, people can look back at 2024 and declare that this was when the field of education entered its new golden era, and our society improved because of it.

Use the tool in figure 1.1 to pause and reflect. In the left column, create a list of four concerns in the field of education that bothered you before the COVID-19 pandemic. In the right column, use your power of vision to vividly describe the transformation that you would like to witness post-pandemic. Be careful not to list issues that simply describe concerns about the behaviors of others (students, parents, and so on); instead, address issues that are within our efficacious control as educators.

Pause to Reflect	
BC (Before COVID)	**AC (After COVID)**

Figure 1.1: Post-pandemic transformation reflection.

*Visit **go.SolutionTree.com/PLCbooks** to download a free reproducible version of this figure.*

Conclusion

The COVID-19 pandemic has made an impression on all our lives, both good and bad. For those of us blessed enough to survive it, this tragedy has produced a unique opportunity to make critical improvements to our lives and our profession during this transition period of uncertainty. It is not enough to go back to the status quo. The pre-COVID reality was not ideal. We experienced declining teacher job satisfaction, unacceptable rates of student failure, and student achievement gaps based on factors like race, income level, home language, and disability. We can do better, and the pathways to a more effective school system existed long before the global pandemic, but the lack of collective efficacy within the field of education allowed us to intellectually admire those better practices without making a full collective commitment to embrace and implement them. I argue that the best of those better pathways is the PLC at Work process. If we dare take another look at this process, which has been around since 1998, we could make the post-COVID era much more promising than the reality before March 2020.

Pause to Think and Plan

Amen!

_____

_____

_____

_____

_____

Aha!

_____

_____

_____

_____

_____

So What?

_____

_____

_____

_____

_____

_____

CHAPTER 2

The Past—How Did We Get Here?

The terms *reforms* and *improvements* are used often when referring to schools and the field of education. We have been trained to look forward, rarely stopping to analyze the history of our sojourn. My experience has taught me that many educators do not know the history of our profession. Perhaps it is wise to take a step back, examine our journey, and use the lessons from the past to guide us into a better future.

There is a symbol used by the Akan people of Ghana called *Sankofa*. The Sankofa symbol is a bird with its head turned backward to capture an egg depicted above its back. The literal meaning of the word *Sankofa* is "to go back and get it." Symbolically, it means taking from the past what is good and bringing it into the present in order to make positive progress through the benevolent use of knowledge (Willis, 1998).

David Tyack and Larry Cuban (1995) affirm that it is not only ineffective but also foolish to think about innovation and educational improvement without a robust reflection on the past:

> History provides a whole storehouse of experiments on dead
> people. Studying such experiments is cheap (no small matter
> when funds are short); and it does not use people (often the poor)
> as live guinea pigs. Many educational problems have deep roots
> in the past, and many solutions have been tried before. If some
> "new" ideas have already been tried, and many have, why not
> see how they fared in the past? (p. 6)

Improvement, innovation, and growth are nothing new to the American school system. These elements have been woven into the fabric of our profession. In many cases, the American education system has been a historic and monumental success, and in others, success has been elusive. It is imperative that we learn from our past, appreciate and celebrate how far we've come, and also collaborate to overcome the obstacles that remain. As this chapter demonstrates, every generation of American citizens and educators has faced a set of critical challenges that they overcame so the system could continue to evolve. Will the current generation of educators be up to the challenge of successfully confronting our modern obstacles?

This chapter begins with an examination of the American school journey so that we can better understand the obstacles we face.

A Retrospective Analysis

Events don't happen in a vacuum; rather, they are the products of the dynamic interaction of multiple factors engaging simultaneously (past, present, and future). American schools have evolved over hundreds of years. Without knowledge of the history of this evolution, we can have only an incomplete perspective—and often a critical lack of gratitude—when making decisions for the future. As we move out of the shadow of the COVID-19 pandemic, this retrospective analysis of the history of education is particularly important.

While we look ahead to the challenge of improving schools, it is important to learn three critical lessons from the past. The first lesson is to understand and stay committed to *purpose*. What drove our society to engage in this massive social experiment known as public schooling, and what benefits did society seek to reap? The second lesson is to review the history of *access*. Unfortunately, discrimination is part of our past, including discrimination along the lines of race, gender, social class, disability, and language. Why have we legally, morally, and professionally constructed barriers to educational access for some students, and what is the history of activism that has made our school system more accessible? The final lesson is to review the history of school *quality*. What is a good education? Is it moral, civic, cognitive? How do you measure it? If we cannot define and agree on quality schooling, then how can we form a positive pathway forward?

Purpose

All human behavior is motivated, calculated, and connected to needs (Ryan & Deci, 2000), and organizations are conduits for fulfilling those needs (McGregor, 1960). Restaurants exist to feed people who are not willing or in a position to cook for themselves. Hotels exist to provide shelter for those who are away from their homes or have a temporary housing need. So, what compelled a society to construct a national network of publicly funded schools? The answer to this question serves as an anchor for our thoughts and actions as we consider our way forward.

Having a common purpose is a powerful catalyst for productivity. Some refer to this as knowing your *why*. Our organization's why is the compelling higher purpose that inspires us and acts as the source of all that we do (Sinek, 2017). I have had the pleasure to travel the globe and work with public school educators all over the world, and I have observed a significant disconnect from the why of education—particularly in the United States. I have seen district leaders, school leaders, and teachers who seem to be more concerned about compliance with policy demands than actual impact on students. I have observed state and federal policymakers who are more concerned about publicly scoring political points and pandering to populist rhetoric than making real substantive educational improvements. I have witnessed parents and community members who seem to be more concerned about the perceived greatness of their own school district than the improvement of the entire system. We as a society seem to be experiencing a disconnect from the original why of our public education system.

Schools are not new, but public schooling is a relatively modern idea. In Europe, before colonization in the Western Hemisphere, schooling and a formal education were privileges of the wealthy and not made accessible to the masses. It should not be surprising, then, that the first documented school within the boundaries of what is now the United States was a private Jesuit school, established in 1565 in St. Augustine, Florida (Kaestle, 1983). However, in the not-too-distant future, a movement to educate the masses would begin with the first glimpse of public schooling—Puritan schools.

PURITAN SCHOOLS

In Massachusetts in 1620, the Puritans introduced the first real glimpse of what would come to be known as public schooling. The Puritans had fled religious persecution in Europe with the goal of migrating to a place where they could practice their faith without government or social hindrance (Cremin, 1957). One of the first acts of service of these religious migrants was to establish a network of schools known as the *Puritan schools*. Why are the Puritan schools worth noting, and why are they foundational to the purpose of American schooling (Pole, 1993)?

- The schools were tuition-free and made available to the masses.

- There was no prequalification for admission.

- They established a curriculum and intentional learning outcomes.

Opening the school experience to the masses would have been considered a major disruption in Europe, but in the new North American colonies, the idea helped form a unique national identity.

This Puritan experiment was not without limitations and questionable motives. It can be argued that the Puritans' motivations were far from altruistic. The curriculum was narrow. The only subject taught was reading, and the only instructional text was the Bible. Additionally, their methods to inspire student engagement were considered, even for the 17th century, abusive:

> Education in the New England colonies was much more religious in nature than in the other colonies. The Puritan influence was strongest here, and one of the primary goals was to teach children (who are inherently bad) how to behave as moral, Christian adults. Schools in New England focused on an understanding of the Bible and the catechisms of the Puritan church; this is illustrated through the passage of the "Ole' Deluder Satan Act" which pushed for literacy among all children. If children could read the Bible, they could steer clear of "that ole' deluder Satan." Discipline was also extremely strict, and sometimes bordered on abuse. (Nelson, 2023)

It is unfair to judge any project on the flaws of the first prototype. The Puritan schools were far from perfect, but they represented a positive move in the right direction.

Analysis of the foundation of public schooling in the United States would not be meaningful without discussing the impact of American education reformer Horace Mann in the 1830s.

HORACE MANN

There is no figure more responsible for advancing the purpose of American public education than Horace Mann. Mann, born into poverty, received a private school education because of the benevolence of a benefactor. He excelled as a student and eventually graduated from Brown University. Mann was moved by the fact that his educational access was the catalyst to his social mobility. This reality drove him to a life of politics and advocacy for a public education system that could provide all children with the type of educational access he was fortunate to have experienced. He was responsible for the establishment of the first public high school, free public schooling for all grade levels, the establishment of a state board of education, and the first statewide system of public education (Chen, 2021). Why are Mann's contributions worth noting and examining as they relate to the purpose of public school?

- Schools as systems were supported economically, socially, and politically by the greater society, not by a sect or a group.
- The curriculum and learning goals were more secular than religious.
- There was an intentional focus on the development of the citizen and the citizen's capacity as a catalyst to the greater social good.
- Mann's work produced a model that could be duplicated nationally and internationally.

Horace Mann set out to produce a system that would cultivate human potential. In the past, this type of system had been accessible only to the wealthy few, and he wanted to make it accessible to all. The public or "common" school was the template for his vision. He referred to this vision as the *great balance wheel of society*. Besides the obvious economic benefits of a more educated populace, Mann recognized schools' potential to be incubators of a more civil society:

> Public schools founded from the 1820s to the 1840s had as a goal the uniting of Americans by instilling in students common moral and political values. It was believed that if all children were exposed to a common instruction in morality and politics,

> the nation might become free of crime, immoral behavior and
> the possibility of political revolution. (Spring, 2022, p. 5)

This "great balance wheel" would make America immune to some social and political ills experienced in Europe and other parts of the world, like bloody revolution. Mann saw schools as the engine of social development and prosperity. These ideas were noble, but we have yet to fully realize them.

Another notable movement in the history of American education is child-centered education.

CHILD-CENTERED EDUCATION

Child-centered education, the idea that the education system should be organized around the needs of the individual child, added another dimension to the evolution of the American public school system. This concept differed from Mann's focus on the school as a means to develop the greater society. Child-centered education introduced the voices of professionals in fields like psychology, sociology, and economics to the field of education. The field began to move from a singular focus on the institution to more of a humanist approach to schooling.

A prominent voice in the movement to center education on the individual needs of the child was Swiss psychologist Jean Piaget. Piaget advocated for the intense study of child brain and social development to tailor the educational experience to each student's specific developmental needs. In *A Piaget Primer: How a Child Thinks*, authors Dorothy G. Singer and Tracey A. Revenson (1978) write:

> Just as Freud has significantly influenced our understanding
> of children's personality development and emotional life,
> so Jean Piaget, the distinguished Swiss psychologist, has
> made enormous contributions to our understanding of their
> intellectual development. His original research ideas have
> resulted in new insights as to how children think, reason, and
> perceive the world—all those mental activities which are labeled
> *cognition*. (pp. 2–3)

Other prominent child-centered education theorists emerged, like Maria Montessori, who proposed five principles of learning: (1) children are shown respect, (2) kids have absorbent minds, (3) sensitive periods are critical for learning, (4) kids learn best in a prepared environment, and (5) kids can teach themselves through auto education (Lillard, 2011). Leaders like Piaget and Montessori challenged the existing paradigm, arguing that the child should be the central focus of the educational process. This was in contrast to Horace Mann's belief that schools should be common and standardized. Mann believed that schools and the students should serve the needs of society. Piaget and Montessori believed that the school system should serve the individual needs of its students.

The debate about the core purpose of American education has been well documented. What is clear is that this experiment known as public schooling has historically been based on the social desire to create a better person, a better society, and a more fulfilled life. I do not believe any dedicated educator could argue with that desired social impact; however, they might argue that our society has been duplicitous, as such liberties were not available to all citizens. Mann's common school vision did not originally include girls, students of color, or students with disabilities (Schement, 2001).

Access

The introduction of public schools launched a great social experiment. Immigrants from Europe dared to challenge the system of economic privilege in their ancestral home and build a new reality of access in their new home. In their attempt to shake off the unpleasant memory of their personal oppression, they themselves created another reality of oppression in their new home—that of exclusion by race, gender, and disability.

RACE

As the Puritans, Thomas Jefferson, and Horace Mann struggled with the concepts of liberty, citizenship, and education for the newly settled European immigrants, they faced some of those same issues with America's Native population. Can a group truly be the torchbearers of liberty but not include the inhabitants of the new land they chose to settle in? This paradox was the subject of robust debate as the American public school system took shape.

Native Americans

The stance of the U.S. government in the 18th and 19th centuries was to eradicate the languages and cultures of the Native Americans and socially integrate them into

American society. This attempt to destroy Native language and culture through schooling was first introduced by Thomas McKenney, the first head of the Office of Indian Affairs. In 1819, the U.S. Congress passed the Civilization Fund Act, which enabled the president of the United States to fund and authorize Christian missionaries to educate Native American children in an attempt to "civilize them into the glory of Anglo-Saxon culture" (Coleman, 1985, p. 35). This legislation led to the development of what were later called *boarding* or *residential schools*. These schools were intentionally constructed outside tribes' reservation lands, and they physically separated children from their parents. The first residential school was the Carlisle Indian School in Carlisle, Pennsylvania, founded in 1879 by Richard Henry Pratt. The slogan for the school was "Kill the Indian, save the man" (Kliewer, Mahmud, & Wayland, 2023). Students were forced to change their Indigenous names; they were not allowed to speak their languages or learn their history. Any attempt to resist the objectives of these institutions could lead to corporal punishment or even death (Reyhner, 2018). The purpose of these residential schools was cultural genocide; instead of being a tool of liberation, schooling was used as a form of tyranny and cultural sterilization.

Thankfully, many Native American nations, tribes, and leaders fought the expansion and perpetuation of the residential school model. The 20th century brought an era of locally run Native schools with the purpose of restoring cultural identification and liberation. This resistance and empowerment movement led to the passage of the Indian Self-Determination and Education Assistance Act, which gave tribes the power to contract with the federal government to run their own independent education systems (Szasz, 1974). As a school consultant, I have had the opportunity to work with many tribal school systems and have witnessed the connection of heritage, culture, and academic excellence these independently run schools can produce. Such legislative victories have been helpful in advancing Native American education, but many challenges still exist. Many locally run Native American school systems struggle to deal with poverty on the reservation, geographic isolation, and recruitment and retaining of qualified teachers (Faircloth, 2020).

African Americans

One of the most controversial contradictions of American idealism is the case of African Americans. At the same time European immigrants fled Europe to settle in North America in search of greater freedom and liberty, they carried with them the European institution of the enslavement of Africans. This contradiction would become the impetus to the American Civil War from 1861 to 1865 between the Northern states, which advocated for the abolishment of slavery, and the Southern states, which seceded from the newly formed nation to preserve the institution of enslavement, a major catalyst to their economy (Masur, 2011). The war ended in 1865 with the abolitionist North as the victors; as a condition of surrender, the Southern states rejoined the American Union. In the aftermath of the war, three constitutional amendments were ratified: the Thirteenth, Fourteenth, and Fifteenth Amendments (Masur, 2011).

Of the three new constitutional amendments, Amendment Fourteen would prove to be the most critical in the education of the newly emancipated former slaves. This amendment guaranteed "equal protection under the laws" for persons "born or naturalized in the United States," and this protection included African Americans. If the Fourteenth Amendment extended equal protection under the law, that would mean all legislation concerning public schooling prior to the Civil War (primarily aimed at White Americans) would be made accessible, by law, to African Americans. James Anderson (1988), professor emeritus of education at the University of Illinois Urbana-Champaign, points out that pre–Civil War, the literacy rate of African Americans was 7 percent, and not long after the Civil War, the literacy rate jumped to nearly 90 percent. Anderson notes that with the help of the federally constructed Freedmen's Bureau, a government agency specifically tasked with supporting the integration of former slaves into American society, schools in the American South had more African American students enrolled than White students by 1880. This new surge of educated African Americans concerned many Whites in the American South, and after the deconstruction of the Freedmen's Bureau in 1872, and the repeal of federal protections for African Americans at the end of the 19th century, the educational progress of African Americans was in great peril (Jones, 2004).

The repeal of local and federal protections for African Americans at the end of the 19th century reached a disturbing peak in 1896 when the U.S. Supreme Court published its decision on a case known as *Plessy v. Ferguson*. The heart of this case was the racial identification of Homer Plessy, who was genetically one-eighth African American and seven-eighths White. The U.S. Supreme Court decided that the government had the right to declare the racial identity of its citizens, and that it was constitutional for laws to be created to segregate racially categorized citizens, as long as that segregation provided equal access to constitutional rights (Groves, 1951). This ruling became known for its approval of the legalization of racial segregation as long as the provisions were "separate but equal." With many federal protections and investments repealed after the early days of antebellum reconstruction, this ruling gave birth to a legal system of racial segregation known as *Jim Crow* (Rist, 1979). Jim Crow laws allowed White politicians to introduce and pass laws that established racial segregation in all public accommodations, including schools, leading to a system that was brutally *separate* and *unequal*.

The legalization of racial segregation in public accommodations led to a massive protest movement known as the American civil rights movement. One of the crowning events of this movement was the U.S. Supreme Court's decision to overturn the *Plessy v. Ferguson* decision with its 1954 ruling in a case known as *Brown v. Board of Education of Topeka*. The case, which was argued by future U.S. Supreme Court justice Thurgood Marshall, affirmed that accommodations by nature cannot be separate and equal (Martin, 2020). The decision concluded that the legal separation of races leads to an inevitable level of inequality (this argument would later be used in undermining the argument to segregate students with disabilities from their peers). This decision ultimately led to the end of legal racial segregation in American schools. Unfortunately, legal decisions cannot change people's values and hearts. When Harvard University reevaluated racial segregation in public schools in America post–*Brown v. Board*, their data concluded that American schools are more segregated in the 21st century than they were before the Supreme Court decision in 1954 (Orfield, 2001). The U.S. Government Accountability Office reports that in the 2020–2021 school year, 18.5 million American students attended a school that was predominantly same race (Ramirez, 2022).

Latinos

Like its history with Native Americans and African Americans, America's history with Latino citizens and students has been complicated and has evolved over time. The ratification of the Treaty of Guadalupe Hidalgo, which ended the Mexican-American War in 1848, would forever change the lives of people in what is now known as the American Southwest. The treaty annexed areas of northern Mexico and made them part of the United States. These states included portions of California, Colorado, New Mexico, Arizona, Utah, and Texas (Guardino, 2017).

The territory annexed into the United States from Mexico sparked a political movement of forced assimilation of Mexicans, similar to the policies of the residential schools for Native Americans. In the immediate aftermath of the Mexican-American War, state governments in the southwest United States tried to use schools to replace the speaking of Spanish with English and to culturally sanitize Mexican American students. In 1856, two years after the Texas legislature established a statewide school system, the government required the mandatory subject of English for all students, and in 1870, the government passed a law requiring that all academic subjects be taught in English (San Miguel, 1987). In states like Colorado, school officials were encouraged to ignore state attendance laws so that local farmers could use Latino students as a source of cheap child labor (Honders, 2017). In 1921, school board members in Ontario, California, openly discussed (on record) building schools along racially stratified lines so that the school population would be exclusively White or Latino. Parents who wanted their children transferred from these intentionally segregated schools unsuccessfully sued the Ontario Board of Education in 1945 under the umbrella of the U.S. Constitution's Fourteenth Amendment (Gonzalez, 1990). The school board argued that the segregation was necessary in order to provide students with specialized instruction in Spanish. In 1946, a U.S. district court judge would rule in the case *Mendez v. Westminster School District of Orange County* that intentional segregation of Latino students based on language was not legally justified nor constitutionally supported. In 1948, a similar case was argued in Texas, *Delgado v. Bastrop Independent School District*, and like in the *Mendez v. Westminster* decision, the courts decided that intentional segregation based on the language or heritage of Latino students was illegal (Gonzales, 2019).

GENDER

Since the 19th century, the struggle for racial and ethnic justice has paralleled the struggle for gender equality. Women organized to secure the ratification of the U.S. Constitution's Nineteenth Amendment in 1920, codifying a woman's right to vote. The struggle for equal rights continued in the 20th century with the development of the National Organization for Women (NOW) in 1966, which successfully lobbied the government to pass one of the most sweeping—and many consider most successful—education reform efforts in U.S. history, Title IX (Lopez, 2003).

Title IX was signed into law in 1972 as part of the Higher Education Act. This law famously states, "No person in the United States shall, on the basis of sex, be excluded from participating in, be denied the benefits of, or be subjected to discrimination under any education program or activity receiving federal financial assistance" (American Association of University Women, 2022). This law applies to all institutions of learning, including preschools, elementary schools, secondary schools, and institutions of higher learning both public and private. In 2014, the federal government updated Title IX protections to include sexual orientation and gender identity (Melnick, 2018).

DISABILITY

In the fight against discrimination and for equal access to an education, very few journeys match the struggle to educate students with disabilities. Prior to the activist movements of the mid-20th century, the need to properly educate physically and mentally disabled students was callously omitted from the national dialogue. Many states ignored the needs of disabled children because of the great expense involved with providing them accommodations for their physical or cognitive needs. In fact, many disabled children were forced to live in state institutions for persons with mental illnesses (Winzer, 1993).

No case illustrates this sad reality for students with disabilities more than what became known as "Allan's Story." Allan was left as an infant by his parents on the steps of an institution for people with intellectual disabilities in the late 1940s. By age thirty-five, Allan had become blind and was frequently observed sitting in the corner of the room slapping his face while rocking back and forth and humming to himself. In the 1970s, Allan was examined and found to be of average intelligence, and it was concluded that his injurious behavior resulted from the environment he had been placed in as an infant (Yell, Rogers, & Rogers, 1998). Stories like Allan's and the activism of parents of children with disabilities launched a full-scale lobbying campaign to have the U.S. government protect the rights of students with disabilities in American public schools.

In 1975, the U.S. Congress passed Public Law 94-142, the Education for All Handicapped Children Act, which guaranteed equal opportunities and support for all students with disabilities. In 1990, the U.S. Congress changed the name of the law to the Individuals With Disabilities Education Act (IDEA). A main provision of this law is a right known as FAPE (Free Appropriate Public Education). Section 300.1(a) of this law states the purpose "to ensure that all children with disabilities have available to them a free appropriate public education that emphasizes special education and related services designed to meet their unique needs and prepare them for further education, employment, and independent living" (U.S. Department of Education, 2017). This provision led to the development of the individual education plan (IEP), which requires schools to create a coordinated strategic approach to meeting the needs of all students covered by IDEA. Laws like Section 504 and the Americans With Disabilities Act were passed to cover students not protected under IDEA (Zirkel & Kincaid, 1995).

Quality

The last frontier of our public school journey is the struggle to define and duplicate excellence. What does an excellent school look like, and how can we duplicate this reality at scale so that every child has access to a quality school? This debate has taken many forms. For our purposes, we will examine three prevalent theories: (1) participation and attendance, (2) moral and character development, and (3) standards and standardized tests.

PARTICIPATION AND ATTENDANCE

The great common school experiment launched by Horace Mann in the 19th century was uncharted territory. Never had a nation tried to educate every member of its society through a national network of free schooling. Passing legislation, creating a framework, funding, and constructing physical facilities were monumental tasks; the system then had to define for itself what successful schooling entailed. An early theory that developed concerning quality schooling was mandatory attendance (Pole, 1993). This premise for having schools be the great balance wheel of society and for giving every student access to the same quality education drove nearly all local and state governments in America to pass compulsory attendance laws for children.

As schools moved into the 20th century, most communities had mandatory attendance laws, but many started to question if mere attendance was an accurate benchmark for assessing the impact of schooling. This question led to the *school graduation movement*, which analyzed school and school district quality based on the number of students who successfully completed their full course of study through twelfth grade, not simply based on attendance (Connell, 1993). This metric also raised concerns because each state and local school board would be empowered to create its own graduation standards. Many questioned if issues like resources, bias, rigor, and opportunities differed from school to school. Authors like Jonathan Kozol (1991) argued that disparities in facilities, learning material, and teacher quality were so great in schools based on race and family income that a metric like high school graduation would essentially be meaningless. He argued that laws and policies governing school funding and investment, like linking school funding to local property taxes, were inherently unfair to communities of color and communities of poverty.

MORAL AND CHARACTER DEVELOPMENT

Another argument levied by Horace Mann in the development of the American public school system was the benefit of moral development. He envisioned that schools would not only provide students with academic benefits but also shape values and character. Is it more important for children to be smart or ethical? In *The Republic and the School*, Lawrence Cremin (1957) points out the context of Mann's school vision in the early 1800s. According to Cremin, this period in American history was a time of mass European migration. Many of the immigrants were fleeing political, religious, or economic persecution in Europe. Most of the children who immigrated had never attended formal school, nor were they prepared to enter the workforce. As a result of these realities, many were getting involved in criminal activity and making cities on the East Coast of the United States unsafe. So it was natural that Mann would appeal to the moral benefits of education, which he envisioned would have a positive effect on social safety.

This sentiment is still prevalent. Since 1966, the year of the mass shooting at the University of Texas, the United States has experienced a staggering increase in mass shootings and gun violence in general. Statisticians have estimated that over 1,200 people have been killed in mass shootings in the United States since 1966, and many of these incidents have happened at schools (Peterson & Densley, 2021). This reality of random violence has caused parents, and society at large, to be concerned about what moral values are being taught in American public schools. One 2014 national poll found that American parents believe moral character is a more important goal of public schooling than academic success (Gewertz, 2014). This issue of violence crosses racial and socioeconomic lines as witnessed in the 2018 mass shooting at Marjory Stoneman Douglas High School, which is nestled in one of the wealthiest residential areas of the state of Florida (Almukhtar, Lai, Singhvi, & Yourish, 2018). It appears that one of the original goals of the public education system was to contribute to the peace and tranquility of society. We have yet to realize that benefit, and we still don't have a consensus on the role that schools play in achieving that end.

STANDARDS AND STANDARDIZED TESTS

By the middle of the 20th century, it was widely accepted that school attendance was not adequate to analyze the impact of schools. This apprehension also extended to high school graduation as the stark differences in school quality and student experiences became more widely documented and there was a public outcry for more tangible evidence of student academic progress (Hamilton, Stecher, & Yuan, 2008). This vacuum in assessing school quality gave birth to the modern academic standards movement. If school attendance alone could not serve as an adequate indicator of school impact, some felt it necessary to define specific learning outcomes (academic standards) and measure them in a standard format (standardized tests) as a measure of school quality across states and nationally. In his book *Beyond Standards: The Fragmentation of*

Education Governance and the Promise of Curriculum Reform, Morgan Polikoff (2021) writes that this approach was problematic in three ways.

1. Who would be empowered to create standards, and would they be nationally adopted?

2. Would standardized measures (tests) be culturally and linguistically appropriate for the social diversity found in American public schools?

3. How would the results of standardized tests be used?

Polikoff (2021) argues that a standards movement would be powerful if these questions were answered with equity in mind. If the criteria for learning success could be clearly defined and assessed, then standards could transcend racial, gender, and socioeconomic biases and other forms of bias by focusing the work of the educator on learning outcomes, not the students' personal characteristics. But this author points out that a movement that appeared to have good intentions (the standards movement) has in many ways diminished school quality and advanced the problem of achievement equity in American schools.

The U.S. federal government has limited authority to enact national education policy. The U.S. Constitution would consider school systems as an extension of states' rights under the Tenth Amendment. In his book *School's In: Federalism and the National Education Agenda*, Paul Manna (2006) describes the delicate dance between the state and federal governments in education policy: "Americans govern their schools with a system as complicated as the country is vast. The nation's fifty states have created nearly 15,000 school districts to oversee nearly 90,000 public schools" (p. 3).

There was an attempt at interstate cooperation in 2006 when former Arizona governor Janet Napolitano, who served as chair of the National Governors Association, successfully garnered the cooperation of forty-one governors to engage in a national standards project that became known as the *Common Core State Standards* (Benchmarks, 2014). There were plenty of controversies surrounding the adoption of these national standards, including perceptions about loss of local control, identification of the threshold of proficiency, and cultural and linguistic bias. The political pressure from citizens at local and national levels caused many states to withdraw from the project, especially after student performance on standardized assessments built around the national standards was far less robust than student performance on previous locally controlled standardized assessments (Urbina, 2010). Creating rigorous and reliable academic standards that would be fair and accurate measures of student learning produces a challenge we are still tackling to this day.

Because the federal government lacks the legal authority to create education policy for fifty different states, it has chosen to exert its influence by leveraging federal school funding to try to create some level of educational alignment. The Elementary and Secondary Education Act (ESEA) of 1965 laid an original blueprint for the federal government's desire for national education. The reauthorization of that law in 2001, which became known as the No Child Left Behind Act (NCLB, 2002), provided federal funds for states to create state academic standards and regularly test students in mathematics and reading, and periodically in science. The law required that, as a condition of federal aid, each state create benchmarks for school passage rates on their standardized tests and create a system of sanctions for schools that did not meet these performance benchmarks. The law also demanded that every school receiving federal aid meet 100 percent student proficiency on state assessments in mathematics and reading by the year 2014 (Melago, 2008). That 100 percent proficiency target was never met, and the law's negative set of consequences for students, educators, and school systems continues to impact schools.

Many researchers found that setting proficiency benchmarks on mandatory standardized academic exams for all public schools did not have a positive impact on student learning, and it created a culture of fear and anxiety among educators (Braun, 2004). In addition to levying these effects on student learning and teacher well-being, punitive standardized testing policies also created an era of cheating on tests, which would lead to criminal charges and arrests for educators in several school systems across the United States (Popham, 2006). Incentivizing schools to collect positive accolades from comparatively high standardized test scores had an economic impact on communities as well—both positive and negative. One study found that a 20 percent increase in standardized state test scores would lead to an estimated 7 percent increase in home values in that community (Card & Rothstein, 2006; Viadero, 2006).

Many educational activists voiced concerns that these state tests were biased culturally, linguistically, and economically and did not accurately measure the intelligence of the student, or the impact of the school and teacher. Studies have consistently shown that these tests are more strongly correlated with school funding, parent education level, and teacher quality than with student intelligence (Couch, Frost, Santiago, & Hilton, 2021). In essence, these tests are more of a measure of the students' environment than of their intelligence or cognitive abilities (Steele, 1997). The fear was that the high-stakes nature of the testing, and the public shaming of schools that did not achieve testing benchmarks, would increase polarization between the haves and have-nots in American society. In 2019, the American Educational Research Association's president went on record at the organization's convention proclaiming testing policies as the "Jim Crow of education" (Jacobson, 2019).

Conclusion

The courageous idealism of the American public school journey is noteworthy and deserving of our respect. This idea of creating a system that would provide educational opportunities to all citizens can be called one of the greatest experiments in human history. It not only disrupted the status quo in the United States but also has been duplicated and advanced in countries all around the world. This movement has not been perfect, and the journey is not yet complete; however, American public education has come a long way from the Puritan schools of the 17th century, and by most accounts, it can be considered a historic and unprecedented success.

Following are the realities of the modern American school system (Riser-Kositsky, 2021). There are:

- 91,328 K–12 public schools
- 32,461 K–12 private schools
- 7,427 K–12 charter schools
- 50.7 million students from multiple ethnicities are enrolled in public schools.
  - ‣ 48.5 percent White
  - ‣ 28 percent Latino
  - ‣ 15 percent African American
  - ‣ 5.4 percent Asian
  - ‣ 0.9 percent Native American
  - ‣ 0.4 percent Pacific Islander

In this chapter, we examined issues concerning the system's *purpose*, *access* to the system, and the need to determine a standard of *quality* that all members of the system can agree on. There have been breakthroughs: the creation of policy, funding, and a system of schooling in every region of the United States. These accomplishments were the result of vision, commitment, and sacrifice from the halls of government to the kitchen tables of every home. The system reflected on some of its limitations of access, and over time, through the work of activists and concerned citizens, deconstructed its laws and policies that hindered access to schooling based on race, gender, and disability. The system has continued to analyze its definition of quality with a realization that physical attendance, graduation rate, and standardized testing might not be fair and reliable methods of assessing school quality. These achievements became reality because people chose to engage and work for the greater good of their society.

As I stated in the introduction of this book, I am concerned that our profession of education, and our society in general, is losing its soul; the journey of public school education is far from complete. Perhaps the PLC at Work process can reinvigorate our professional soul and help us meet the standard of activism modeled in generations past. I am concerned that we might be the first generation of educators to lie down in the face of their modern challenges. Imagine if generations past had accepted racial segregation, gender exclusion, and mistreatment of students with disabilities. What if they had been consumed with their personal struggles and accepted that the challenges of their time were the responsibility of someone else? Would we have the desegregated schools, gender protections, and disability accommodations that we take for granted today? We will never know, because brave individuals advocated for equity in education, and we are the beneficiaries of their courage. As in the previous chapter, take some time to reflect on your plans to respond to the challenges posed in this chapter.

In the next chapter, I will vividly describe the contemporary challenges that we face in the field of education. These challenges include confronting the impact of the COVID-19 pandemic on both students and educators, social and political divisions that impact educational policy, and academic achievement gaps that have become more intense since 2020. Will we rise to the professional challenges of our generation?

Pause to Think and Plan

Amen!

Aha!

So What?

CHAPTER 3

The Present—Where Are We Now?

The COVID-19 pandemic brought the predictability of daily life for people around the world to an abrupt halt in March 2020. Like most people, I tried to create a new routine during the shelter-in-place lockdown. Some days, I viewed the quarantine as a blessing. Perhaps I needed this brief disruption to my hectic life and filled-to-the-brim calendar. Other days, I viewed quarantine as torture. The consistently conflicting reports in the media about how and when the pandemic would end were maddening. I was stuck in this state of malaise, and I had no clue when it would end. I was not alone in my feelings of despair.

As I, like many others, struggled with my well-being during the pandemic quarantine, I grew concerned about how the school system would respond to the gravity of the moment. Nearly fifty-one million American children were ordered to stay at home and finish the 2019–2020 school year there (Education Week Staff, 2021). This seemed like a temporary inconvenience, but as it became more apparent that the pandemic restrictions would last beyond a short window of time, I and others became more worried about the long-term strategy for schools.

In April 2020, as the immediate future of society and schools appeared uncertain, prominent educational scholar John Hattie (2020) published his article "Visible Learning Effect Sizes When Schools Are Closed: What Matters and What Does Not." Hattie, who is famous for his comprehensive meta-analyses and body of research, mapped out what years of research have shown to be the best responses to schooling when schools are closed for long periods of time. In the article, he points out that no body of literature addressed pandemic quarantines specifically, but there has been a rich history of studies concerning long-term school closures because of volcanoes, wildfires, and other natural disasters. In essence, students' missing long stretches of school due to circumstances beyond their control is not new, and we have evidence about what is likely to have a positive impact on student learning in this context. Some of Hattie's (2020) major findings and recommendations include the following.

- Not all school closures are the same. Holidays or extended breaks are normal and are meant for recharging and enrichment. They are not the same as extended breaks due to disasters, which can produce anxiety and uncertainty and can negatively impact student and teacher engagement.

- Technology is a medium only. Research has shown that technology alone has a small impact on student learning. What is more important is how the medium is being used by the teacher and the learner.

- Home conditions greatly impact student learning. Both parent education level and home communication have a strong impact on student learning. If students are going to be quarantined from teachers for long periods of time, it is important that teachers tailor distance learning in the knowledge that not all students have highly educated parents to support them.

- Positive student relationships become more important during virtual learning. The teacher has no direct influence on student participation, unlike in face-to-face instruction. These relationships are even more important in pandemic-induced virtual learning because of the stress and anxiety teachers, students, and parents experience. This is not the time to engage in frivolous power struggles.

- Direct instruction almost totally loses its traditional impact on student learning in the virtual format. Face time between teacher and student is not a big priority in virtual learning. Students should be engaged in tasks at home or virtually that are more constructivist in nature and stimulate higher-order thinking.

- Teachers should limit the scope of their intended learning objectives and focus only on curricular standards that are essential.

- Teachers should check for understanding frequently and even consider eliminating traditional grading practices. The feedback must be timely, and the student should have adequate opportunity to process the feedback, respond to it, and improve based on it.

- Teachers should secure time to provide students with targeted feedback and provide direct intervention for students based on that feedback.

An interesting fact about Hattie's (2020) recommendations is that many of them are tenets of the PLC at Work process, which are cornerstones of good practice at any time—not just when schools are closed. Hattie's recommendations emphasize things like limited unnecessary learning objectives, frequent formative assessments, and an intentional focus on direct support for students based on the evidence of learning. Unfortunately, the systemic response to school closures at the school district, state, and federal levels did not embrace Hattie's recommendations and insights.

The systemic response to COVID-19 pandemic education was greatly polarized in the United States, and that polarization was usually along political and ideological lines. Policies tended to be created around populist sentiment rather than sound education research. One study found that in states where *closed-shop* labor laws existed (states where workers have to join a union if there is a collective bargaining agreement) and where teachers' union treasuries were in the top fifth nationally, schools were nearly two times less likely to begin the 2020–2021 or 2021–2022 school year in person compared to schools in states with *right-to-work* laws (states where workers have the option not to join a workplace union, even if there is a collective bargaining agreement) and poorly funded teachers' unions (Marianno, Hemphill, Loures-Elias, Garcia, Cooper, & Coombes, 2022). This study found that this push for totally virtual instruction was fueled by teachers' fear of contracting COVID-19 and school officials' greater power and control over their workday and teaching conditions. Another study found that the state's preference for president in the 2020 election had a strong correlation with their likelihood of adopting an in-person school model for the 2020–2021 school year. States supporting the Republican presidential candidate spent on average 871.9 hours in in-person schooling compared to 440.2 hours for states supporting the Democratic presidential candidate during the 2020–2021 school year (Lehrer-Small,

2021). This research shows that populist politics had more influence over education policy than empirical research did. This clash of culture and politics weighed heavily on educators during the COVID-19 pandemic lockdown, and it continues to affect our way forward, as I address later in this chapter.

The PLC at Work process is just good practice. We knew this fact before, during, and after the COVID-19 pandemic. Many researchers, like John Hattie, tried to give us insight into ways to mitigate the educational impact of pandemic education, but unfortunately, many people did not listen. We have the freedom of choice, but we are not free of the consequences of those choices. I will explore what the tangible impact of ignoring sound research is and why PLC at Work is more important now than at any other time in our journey as a profession.

The Psychological Effects of COVID-19 on Educators

As an author and school consultant, I work directly and indirectly with schools. My work as an author provides educators with written support for school improvement, but most of my work time is spent in direct physical support of educators—either through professional development or coaching on their school campuses or through interactions at workshops and conferences. After the U.S. government's restrictions on face-to-face interaction became policy in late March 2020, workshops and conferences were no longer possible. For many in my line of work, teacher training and support turned to Zoom and other videoconferencing platforms in an attempt to address the enormous new challenges educators were facing while trying to serve students remotely.

A challenge of virtual instruction is the limitation it introduces for engagement. At best, direct virtual instruction during a workshop or online training can be three dimensional.

1. **Using sight:** Participants see one another physically through a live stream using their web cameras.

2. **Using sound:** Participants hear one another through the audio stream.

3. **Using writing:** Participants share their thoughts in writing through the chat or writing feature of the videoconferencing platform.

These three dimensions are possible if all participants use the videoconferencing features. What often happened in reality fell well short of this description. Often, participants attended reluctantly, and since no protocol for engagement in virtual learning was developed before COVID-19, it was common for participants to (1) never turn on their video camera so you never knew if they were present, (2) mute their audio feature and never say a word for the entire experience, and (3) never use the chat feature to share thoughts and impressions in writing. In many instances on Zoom, I did not know if I was talking to anyone but myself. This new reality was frustrating to me as a teacher of adults; I was seeking to make a difference and have a positive impact, and I did not know if my efforts were in vain. The uncertainty of each virtual training experience left me to wonder if it was going to be three, two, one, or zero dimensional, which affected my energy and mood as a professional. As these schools started to partially reopen and I got an opportunity to see the effect that this conundrum had on teachers using this platform with students each day, I was not surprised about its negative emotional and physical impact on educators, which was similar to my personal experience.

Schools that did not choose totally virtual instruction had the option to allow students to come to school if they applied the Centers for Disease Control and Prevention's (CDC's) social-distancing and sanitation standards. Most of these schools required teachers and students to wear masks and stay six feet or farther apart (Frick, 2020). Schools were not physically built for this type of spatial proximity, so it caused management and engagement nightmares. Teachers reported that they spent a large portion of their day convincing students to keep their masks over their nose and mouth, sanitizing classrooms, taking student temperatures, and looking for students or colleagues who showed signs of illness (Schwartz, 2021b). Schools that chose in-person instruction during the pandemic commonly had massive COVID-19 spread and shut down for days and weeks at a time. One report found that there were over 1,400 school closures during the 2020–2021 school year due to COVID-19 outbreaks among the school staff and students (Camera, 2021).

In March 2021, I had the opportunity to conduct a rare in-person professional development at a school. The pandemic restrictions had been our collective reality for a full year, and the norms of social distancing, masking, and constant sanitization had become everyone's new normal. The workshop began at 8:00 a.m. in the school library. The first participants slowly started to trickle into the library around 7:58 a.m., the administrators arrived around 8:07 a.m., and the rest of the faculty made it to the library by 8:16 a.m. Unfortunately, late starts are not unusual for school professional development, but the energy and the body language were different from what I experienced pre-pandemic. We finally started the workshop around 8:20 a.m., and the low energy and looks of despair were evident on the faces of all the participants. They looked as if they had all experienced a collective trauma. I spent the first hour of the full-day workshop just trying to put smiles on their faces through a few lighthearted activities. They looked as if they were all at the ends of their ropes, so I finally stopped and asked, "How do you feel, honestly?" A veteran teacher stood and said with tears in her eyes, "Dr. Muhammad, this has been the worst year of my teaching career. I leave here daily, and I don't know if I can wake up and return the next day. I have loved being a teacher for twenty-eight years, and this has by far been my most unenjoyable year of teaching. *Something just feels different!*"

Had we proceeded with these modified forms of schooling without deep consideration for the impact that these experiences would have on teachers, students, parents, and the community at large? Had we totally ignored the empirical evidence Hattie (2020) and others had shared about the best way to proceed through this abnormal window of time?

An article published in the *Journal of Family Medicine and Primary Care* in October 2020 (Jain, Bodicherla, Raza, & Sahu, 2020) expressed alarming concerns about the psychological effects of COVID-19, specifically three primary concerns about the emerging impact of the COVID-19 quarantine on mental health.

1. Increased anxiety about personally contracting COVID-19 or having a vulnerable loved one contract it

2. Increased panic over misinformation shared on social media or in questionable primary or secondary sources

3. Post-traumatic stress disorder (PTSD) that could emerge after the quarantine and might have long-term ramifications for human-to-human interactions after pandemic restrictions were lifted

These concerns were validated as the quarantine restrictions remained in place for nearly two years. KFF, formerly known as the Kaiser Family Foundation, found that the percentage of American adults reporting signs of anxiety or depression or both increased from 11 percent to 41.1 percent between 2019 and 2021 (Panchal, Saunders, & Rudowitz, 2023).

In the late spring or early summer of 2020, it became apparent that most of America's public schools would move to a virtual learning model; the vast majority of educators were untrained in this new medium of teaching, and school districts transitioned their entire learning platforms in a matter of months (Baker, 2022). To make matters worse, legislators were making decisions about virtual learning requirements with less experience and insight in classroom teaching than most teachers had.

Many states required teachers and students to simulate the conditions of face-to-face learning through videoconferencing platforms. As John Hattie (2020) found, direct instruction almost totally loses its traditional impact on learning on a virtual platform. This decision to attempt to simulate face-to-face learning conditions virtually was unwise without proper preparation for the use of this technology and effective pedagogy on this platform. Devin Vodicka (2020) makes the following two assertions in his book *Learner-Centered Leadership: A Blueprint for Transformational Change in Learning Communities.*

1. Seat time is an antiquated and unreliable measure of educational effectiveness.

2. Distance learning makes seat-time requirements nearly impossible because of the negative effects on the student and the teacher.

The illogical and polarized responses of politicians, the stress on converting learning activities to a virtual platform, and the personal fear and anxiety of living through a pandemic and teaching students in person under CDC guidelines had devastating effects on educators' individual and collective psyches. According to psychology professor Serge Doublet (2000), stress has a debilitating psychological effect on human beings. When people improperly process stress, they tend to gravitate toward others to vent their discontent and validate their behavioral reactions. Instead of leaning into the advice and empirical research, many educators turned to one another to vent and seek validation of their dissatisfaction with pandemic education. No platform served as a greater host to this activity than social media. A 2022 study found that teachers' professional and social habits changed significantly during pandemic education; their social interaction habits were negatively impacted in three ways (Jones, Camburn, Kelcey, & Quintero, 2022).

1. The distancing requirements made it difficult to engage in physical human interaction and created social isolation among peers.

2. The struggle of virtual instruction or mitigated face-to-face instruction raised professional anxiety and stress.

3. Social media became an outlet to share professional frustration, and social media algorithms matched frustrated educators with thousands of others experiencing the same stress and anxiety.

The study found that these three realities resulted in higher rates of teacher sick days, resignations, and generally unpleasant behavior, like irritability and impatience, during the pandemic. This might help explain what I witnessed firsthand in the school library in March 2021.

Trying to educate young people—in any era—is challenging. Venting to colleagues about general workplace stress is considered a natural part of most workplace cultures. In a book I coauthored with Sharroky Hollie (Muhammad & Hollie, 2012), *The Will to Lead, the Skill to Teach*, I warned that this inclination toward venting and complaining is problematic because healthy school cultures tend to gravitate toward collaborative problem solving and pragmatism. Given what we know about the psychological impact of COVID-19, this habit has become even more problematic in today's context. In a 2018 *Harvard Business Review* article titled "Stop Complaining About Your Colleagues Behind Their Backs," author Deborah Grayson Riegel (2018) points out that complaining behavior can destroy organizational culture. She asks the reader if they have ever been on what she calls a "confirmation expedition." According to Riegel, a confirmation expedition happens when we engage in one of two experiences.

1. We ask a colleague to confirm our own negative or challenging experience with a third colleague who is not present.

2. We welcome a similar line of confirmation inquiry from a colleague about a third colleague who is not present.

With our current access to social media and social connections to people all around the world, what used to be an isolated set of toxic exchanges in a school's teachers' lounge has now grown into a global network of workplace toxicity.

Besides the general feeling of unease, a culture of complaining and workplace gossip has a concrete set of negative ramifications. In their journal article "Passing the Word: Toward a Model of Gossip and Power in the Workplace," Nancy B. Kurland and Lisa Hope Pelled (2000) define *gossip* as "informal and evaluative talk in an organization, usually among no more than a few individuals, about another member of that organization who is not present" (p. 429). This cultural habit can have the following effects on workplace culture.

- Erosion of trust

- Hurt feelings

- Low morale

- Damaged reputations

- Reduced personal and professional credibility

- Increased anxiety and divisiveness

- Attrition

Kurland and Pelled (2020) point out that the desire to have others validate our position can be described as destructively addictive. The need to be right, and find others to validate one's perspective, stimulates the body's production of adrenaline and dopamine (chemical rewards) and affirms to the individual that they're OK. These two powerful chemical agents provide a reward for narrow-mindedness and an aversion to cognitive dissonance, which can be counterproductive to personal and professional growth (Glaser, 2013). These issues were already problematic before COVID-19, but were greatly enhanced by the stress and challenge of a job that becomes more challenging every day.

Dopamine and adrenaline, which are produced when finding comfort in those experiencing the same struggle, can feel rewarding, but other chemical, physical, and emotional reactions related to constant complaining can be much less beneficial. Like the veteran teacher I observed in the library in the spring of 2021, many educators have reported feeling mentally, physically, and emotionally tired since March 2020. Stanford University published a study in 2016 that assessed complaining's cognitive, physical, and chemical impacts on a person (Bradberry, 2016). The study concluded that constant complaining has the following impacts.

- Habitual complaining produces a default neurological bridge to the amygdala (the emotional center of the brain), which causes the brain to habitually respond to frustration emotionally as opposed to pragmatically.

- Habitual complaining vastly increases the body's production of cortisol (a stress hormone).

- Habitual complaining shrinks the hippocampus, which negatively impacts memory and the ability to learn.

Access to social media platforms and their ability to link like-minded thinkers created a level of complaining and professional vitriol that I had not witnessed before the traumatic experience of COVID-19 and pandemic education. Many social media posts I observed from educators expressed anger, distress, and hopelessness. These educators were frustrated by students, parents, administrators, the government, and society at large. It was difficult to witness so many good, ethical people seemingly stuck in this downward emotional spiral. Mental health writer Andrea Darcy (2023) describes this as the *victim mentality*: "when we have a victim mentality, we see the world through a lens of good versus bad. We are the innocent person, and the bad things are outside of ourselves." Darcy asserts that the victim mentality is a misunderstood and counterproductive coping mechanism for stress and that a psychologically healthy person "sees that they are choosing what is happening to them and sees their power to take charge." Why is this important? As discussed previously, advocacy for the survival and vibrance of the public education system has a long history that includes challenges for economic, racial, gender, and disability inclusion and equity. Historically, educators' response has been to strategize, act, and efficaciously organize to leverage their collective impact on the system to make it better. If we are experiencing some degree of collective victim mentality, will we be able to efficaciously improve the system and its modern challenges?

How is all of this affecting teachers today? The evidence is daunting. A Merrimack College study published in April 2022 shows that the COVID-19 pandemic's impact on teacher mental health and job satisfaction was as bad as anyone could have imagined (Will, 2022a). The study found that teacher job satisfaction in April 2022 was as low as it has ever been in the history of public education, with a national job satisfaction rate of 12 percent. This means that eighty-eight out of every hundred American teachers were deeply dissatisfied with their jobs. This is not the recipe for a positive way forward. The top four reasons for job dissatisfaction are as follows.

1. Poor and inadequate compensation

2. Increased social and emotional needs of students

3. Public criticism and vilification of teachers and the teaching profession

4. Being stretched too thin

All the issues the study highlights can be resolved when reasonable people sit down, collaborate, listen to one another, and seek mutually beneficial solutions. But with political and social polarization, deep evidence of educator despair, and the unresolved psychological impact of COVID-19 on everyone, these issues will require an unusual level of grit and altruism. These are challenges that we must face and overcome.

The Tangible Effects of COVID-19 on the School System

It would be nearly impossible for a society to endure the kind of unprecedented stress caused by COVID-19 and not experience tangible negative effects. Society experienced increases in long-term health challenges, unemployment, violent crime, hyperinflation, and business closures (El-Sadr, Vasan, & El-Mohandes, 2023). Other effects of the pandemic were more deliberate, like what became known as the "Great Resignation."

In October 2022, about four million American workers—2.6 percent of the total American workforce—voluntarily quit their jobs according to a study published by the World Economic Forum (Ellerbeck, 2023). This study found the following top three reasons for this mass resignation.

1. Low pay

2. No opportunities for advancement

3. Feeling disrespected

These factors are eerily similar to the drivers of low morale among teachers identified in the Merrimack College study (Will, 2022a). Unfortunately, the Great Resignation has had an enormous impact on the teacher workforce.

A combination of teacher resignations, a lack of newly certified teachers entering the workforce, and uninformed public policies to staff America's schools, which lower the requirements to enter the teaching profession, serve as big threats to the improvement and longevity of the public school system. The current teacher shortage is real and serves as an immediate threat to school quality. Kansas State University found that to start the 2022–2023 school year, there were over 36,500 unfilled teaching vacancies in American public schools (Will, 2022b). Not only did the 2022–2023 school year start with an unprecedented number of teacher vacancies, but also 163,350 vacancies were filled with uncertified teachers, substitute teachers, or teachers certified in an area other than their assigned teaching position. This report notes that the majority of these instances were occurring in urban or rural school systems. To affirm this point about the disproportionate distribution of vacancies and uncertified teachers in urban and rural school districts, Chicago Public Schools, one of America's largest urban school districts, experienced an 85 percent increase in employee resignations in the first seven months of the 2021–2022 school year compared to the previous school year (Koumpilova, 2022). These resignations were not limited to teachers, but included central office administrators, school administrators, and nonteaching staff.

A story that encapsulates the gravity of educators' Great Resignation is that of a teacher who quit her job in December 2022 and posted a resignation video on the social media platform TikTok under the name Millennial Ms. Frizzle (Lenzen, 2022). The video accumulated over two million views in the first week after it was posted. This former teacher, who quit her teaching job to work at the wholesale grocer Costco, went viral because of her apparent increase in mood, energy, and optimism since leaving her teaching job. She states in the video:

> I used to be a teacher, and now I work at Costco. This is my first ever year not having a winter break. And how do I feel? I feel great. Just worked Christmas Eve. . . . I just worked seven days straight, including Christmas Eve, and I feel fine. (Lenzen, 2022)

We are amid a serious crisis in our profession when a low-wage, entry-level job becomes a more attractive option than teaching America's children.

Of course the issues of teacher resignation, teacher discontent, and teacher labor shortages predate COVID-19 (Sutcher, Darling-Hammond, & Carver-Thomas, 2016), but the evidence is clear that the strain of the pandemic turned a dire situation from bad to worse. The strain of COVID-19 caused a national Great Resignation that has affected nearly every field, and the field of education also simultaneously experienced a massive decrease in the supply of new teachers preparing to enter the profession. According to one report, the number of new teachers being prepared in traditional four-year university credentialing programs has decreased by nearly 30 percent since 2010 (Goldhaber & Holden, 2020). This report points out that there was a slight uptick in new teacher preparation in 2019, compared to the previous nine years, but that uptick immediately vanished after the onset of the COVID-19 pandemic in 2020, primarily because many students had to complete their student teaching requirements virtually or finish their college coursework online. Many students in teacher education programs did not find these options professionally or financially advantageous, and dropped out or delayed their certification completion.

Education analyst Chad Aldeman (2022) identifies six reasons why there has been a massive decline in university students' interest in becoming traditionally certified teachers.

1. COVID-related changes have made teaching less enjoyable.

2. Book bans, the fight over critical race theory, and culture wars have made teaching more political. (I will address this issue later in this chapter.)

3. Respect for teachers has declined.

4. Starting salaries are too low.

5. Increased certification and licensing requirements (certification exams) have made the profession less attractive to potential teachers.

6. Broader economic opportunities and more potential career choices have developed.

According to Aldeman (2022), the combination of these realities has been the catalyst to an alarming shortage of licensed teachers, and this issue appears to affect the students who have traditionally been disadvantaged the most.

With regard to school funding, racial and gender segregation, and students with disabilities, we could traditionally depend on the government to be an important partner in addressing educational crises through funding, legal decisions, and public policy (for example, Title IX and IDEA). It appears that in the current context, this traditional partnership might be seriously compromised or in total jeopardy. In the 1980s, when Finland looked to forge a better future for its citizens, it placed educational excellence at the center of its strategy. This investment created a rigorous and honorable educational pathway to the profession, which included a master's degree as a minimum requirement for entry into the teaching profession, a lengthy and intense internship under the guidance of a master teacher, strong investment in collaboration and continued professional growth, and among the top wages in Finland (Sahlberg, 2021). This national investment in the development and preparation of teachers, teacher salary, and national respect for the teaching profession has led Finland to become one of the leading models in the world for effective public education. The U.S. government has chosen a very different route.

In June 2022, Florida governor Ron DeSantis signed into law a policy that allows military veterans to teach in Florida schools without a teacher license or college degree (Riddell & Arundel, 2022). The requirements of this teaching certification waiver include that the veteran have at least forty-eight months of military service with an honorable or medical discharge and that the hiring school district assign the new hire an experienced teacher mentor. The law places no restrictions on academic subjects or grade-level requirements for this teaching certification. The passage of this law immediately caused grave concern among school leaders in the state of Florida. One Florida school administrator was reported as saying that a potential solution to a statewide teacher shortage issue has education leaders feeling as though [Governor Ron DeSantis's] administration is undermining the qualifications of classroom instructors (Harrell, 2022). A teachers' union president asserted that she respects the service of the military veterans, but the skills needed to successfully teach a student are different from the skills required to be successful on the battlefield. Unfortunately, Florida was not alone in its haste to fill teaching vacancies. The state of Arizona passed a similar law known as SB 1159 (Joyce, 2022). This law does not require that a new teacher in Arizona fulfill the state's traditional legal requirements for being a certified teacher, which include obtaining a bachelor's degree in education, doing student teaching, and passing the state's written certification exam. Under this law, the newly commissioned teacher only has to provide proof of enrollment in a teacher certification program.

It is difficult to sustain a quality public school system without well-qualified teachers. Like other professionals, teachers want to be paid a fair wage, work in fair conditions, and be supported in their endeavor to be successful at their craft. The concerns about the workforce existed before COVID-19, but the pandemic has accelerated the negative trend. This is a challenge that can be overcome with thoughtful collaboration about policy, proper investments, and a positive attitude. I am concerned that without a thoughtful pivot, these realities will continue to trend in the wrong direction.

The Psychological Effects of COVID-19 on Students

If responding to the disruption of COVID-19 was difficult for adults, there can be no doubt about the strain that the pandemic had on students. How did students respond to social isolation, virtual instruction, CDC guidelines in schools, and loss of nonacademic activities? In my interactions with educators since March 2020, it is rare that these topics don't arise. If we are going to move forward to unprecedented heights of public school effectiveness, we will have to examine and respond to the pandemic's effect on students with the same level of veracity that we discuss and respond to the impact on educators.

A prevalent narrative that I have experienced in my work with educators since March 2020 is frustration with students' attention span, impulse control, compliance with structure, academic skill level, and apathy. As I've worked in schools since the onset of the pandemic, I have witnessed evidence of teachers' real frustration. In late 2021, I was conducting a coaching session with a middle school leadership team. The session was relatively productive, but I felt more like a therapist than a leadership coach. As I tried to swing the conversation to tangible matters like performance data, policy, and SMART goal creation, a member of the team would always find a way to interject into the conversation an issue they were flabbergasted about related to students. The stimulation of the amygdala to complain as described in Stanford University's study (Bradberry, 2016) was in full effect. Finally, one team member, who appeared to be at his wit's end, stated, "Dr. Muhammad, I really can't process what you are sharing because we are in survival mode! Under normal circumstances, I would be fully engaged, but these are not normal circumstances; *the kids are different*!"

This educator's thought was on my radar—I had been hearing similar thoughts in the months that preceded my interaction with the educators at this middle school—but it had never been expressed so clearly to me before.

We have known for years that traumatic experiences have adverse effects on children, both cognitively and emotionally. These experiences have traditionally included things like divorce, bullying, poverty, and molestation. Some refer to these experiences as *adverse childhood experiences* (Hudson, 2005). Mental health professionals in and out of schools have studied these incidents and created infrastructure in response to them. However, I do not know that educators or mental health professionals were prepared to respond to the cognitive and psychological impact that a global pandemic, virtual or mitigated in-person schooling, and social media would have on children over a two-year period.

We know that the COVID-19 pandemic had devastating effects on children. First, the shelter-in-place orders and destabilization of school routine caused adverse childhood experiences for nearly all children. This experience cut across racial, cultural, and socioeconomic lines nationwide. Wealth and privilege did not shield anyone from the restrictions levied by COVID-19 policy. One study found that the anxiety caused by the abrupt halt of all social activities (shelter in place) had devastating consequences for adolescents, causing their brains to age years in a matter of months (Sparks, 2022b). Another major study focused on the reaction of two hundred adolescents (between ages nine and fifteen) in Santa Clara, California, who were experiencing shelter-in-place orders and virtual schooling between the summer of 2020 and 2021 (Gotlib et al., 2022). The study also monitored the social media habits of these two hundred adolescents during the span of the study. The results were not only shocking to the public, but shocking to the researchers.

- The impact of isolation caused a dangerously elevated level of anxiety, especially for participants actively involved in social media consumption for two or more hours per day.

- The impact of isolation caused major damage to the development of the cerebral cortex, the part of the brain that governs memory, thinking, learning, reasoning, and problem solving.

- Anxiety and cognitive damage appeared to be more severe in low-income households.

Not only did the pandemic make children's brains age prematurely, but it also caused major cognitive damage in parts of the brain that are critical to school function, especially for students of poverty.

We have learned that COVID-19 and social isolation caused some lingering cognitive damage for students, but it also had a devastating effect on them socially and emotionally. When I think about my experience in school as a child, my fondest memories come from activities that were primarily nonacademic. I remember the games played at recess and field trips in elementary school. I remember laughing with my friends during lunch and passing notes to girls I liked in middle school. I remember interscholastic sports, homecoming, senior skip day, and the prom in high school. For nearly two years during the COVID-19 pandemic, whether schooling was virtual or in person with restrictions, most students did not get an opportunity to have those same experiences. Georgetown University found that these restrictions had a major impact on the emotional and social development of children (Natanson & Meckler, 2020). Missing out on these major experiences in a child's socialization caused many students to experience anger and withdrawal.

From my review of the research, the most common and potentially most devastating legacy of COVID-19 for students is the skyrocketing rates of anxiety and depression. Earlier in the chapter, I shared some data on the increase in anxiety and depression among American adults during the pandemic; the rates for children were far worse. A telling study on this topic was commissioned by the nonprofit organization YouthTruth (YouthTruth Student Survey, 2022). This comprehensive study included 222,837 students from 845 schools across 20 U.S. states. The results were troubling.

- Anxiety, stress, and depression were the top concerns of students involved in this study.

- Fifty percent of middle school students and 56 percent of high school students reported consistent feelings of stress, anxiety, or depression.

- Anxiety and depression were twice as likely for students whose families lived at or below the national poverty line. This disparity existed primarily because of the increased financial strain on families during the pandemic, which caused events like food and housing insecurity not experienced by high-wage earners. Children of poverty were also more likely to experience the death of a loved one caused by COVID-19.

- Girls were more likely to feel anxiety and depression than boys, and LGBTQ youth of all genders were more at risk for anxiety and depression than non-LGBTQ youth. The study found that increased social media exposure during shelter-in-place or virtual schooling had a greater negative impact on girls and LGBTQ students and may explain the disparity.

- Nearly 80 percent of the students with feelings of anxiety and depression shared that they could not find help for their condition at school, and they often felt the impatience and rigidity of school staff (for example, grading deadlines and school rules) made the feelings worse.

Educator assessments are correct: *these kids are different.* They have experienced things that no generation before them endured. The most alarming part of the YouthTruth study, in my assessment, is the fact that most youths experiencing these emotional struggles find that school professionals not only are unhelpful but are more than likely to worsen the symptoms, making school even less attractive.

The Tangible Effects of COVID-19 on Students

We are still uncovering the personal and psychological impact of the COVID-19 pandemic on society as a whole and students specifically. Scientists and researchers are uncovering new critical findings all the time. It will take us years to fully understand the impact made by such an unprecedented event. What tangible effects has the COVID-19 pandemic had on the process of schooling? Based on the research shared in this chapter, it shouldn't surprise us that one study found that 70 percent of American schools reported a significant increase in chronic absenteeism for students compared to pre-pandemic numbers (Sparks, 2022a). For nearly two years, students became accustomed to not attending school or infrequently attending school. Another study found that it would have been wise for school districts to acclimate students back to the normalcy of schooling instead of abruptly reconvening pre-pandemic norms; instead, school districts turned to gimmicks like gift cards to bribe students into attending school, with little evidence of effectiveness (Fortin, 2022). In addition to experiencing an increase in absenteeism, schools have alarmingly increased their identification of African American boys as being in need of special education services. A study commissioned by two nonprofit organizations, Bellwether and Easterseals, found that since 2019, the rate of placing African American boys in special education has increased by nearly 20 percent (Hinds, Newby, & Korman, 2022). The study found that teacher stress (mainly due to the pandemic), teacher impatience, poor systems of support in school, and an implicit bias against Black males are the major causes of this increase in special education placement. Studies have shown that getting placed in special education makes a student more likely to be denied access to grade-level-appropriate curriculum (Loveless, 2013), and the likelihood of dropping out of school drastically increases for African American boys assigned to special education (Sullivan & Bal, 2013).

In addition to having devastating cognitive and emotional effects on students, COVID-19 had negative effects on their academic progress. The policy decisions about whether to have virtual or in-person learning during the pandemic were based not on sound research but on a series of factors unrelated to quality schooling (like politics and labor influence). A review of the literature shows that all students struggled and fell behind in their learning progression during the pandemic, but those who received schooling exclusively through a virtual platform fared worst (Schwartz, 2022b). One study found that all students demonstrated small growth, compared to previous years, in mathematics during the 2020–2021 school year, but Black and Latino students regressed significantly in reading as well (Halloran, Jack, Okun, & Oster, 2021). This study relied heavily on a privately administered national assessment known as the Measures of Academic Progress (MAP) to analyze student progress. The assessment is administered online, and the study is careful to note that the negative impact on Black and Latino students might be higher than the study projects because nearly 25 percent of those students did not log in to the assessment portal and take the exam. The reality of making policy decisions based primarily on populist politics instead of empirical evidence is that a poor decision can have a devastating long-term impact.

Harvard University's Center for Education Policy Research released a study in 2022 that provided a national analysis of the effects of pandemic education (Goldhaber, Kane, McEachin, Morton, Patterson, & Staiger, 2022). This Harvard study found that on average for the 2020–2021 and 2021–2022 school years, American students made about 80 percent of the academic progress they would typically make during a school year pre-pandemic. The researchers refer to this gap in typical progress as *unfinished learning*. Harvard found that unfinished learning was especially high for students who received instruction exclusively on a virtual platform, and the unfinished learning for students of poverty experiencing only virtual instruction was triple the national rate. This study suggests that schools intentionally set aside funding for at least three years to intentionally identify and support students to recover the learning they lost due to the pandemic.

In October 2022, we received the most definitive evidence of student learning loss during the pandemic. The U.S. Department of Education periodically administers a test called the National Assessment of Educational Progress (NAEP) across all fifty U.S. states. This assessment is also referred to as the *Nation's Report Card* because it is considered the most comprehensive and valid assessment of learning trends across the country (Viadero, 2010). The assessment has been administered to a sample of students all across the United States since 1969. Most anticipated that the results would not be flattering or encouraging. Here's what the 2022 NAEP results revealed.

- Nationally, there was a 3 percent drop in fourth- and eighth-grade students' reading proficiency test performance from 2019 to 2022.

- Nationally, there was a 5 percent drop in fourth-grade students' mathematics proficiency test performance and an 8 percent drop in eighth-grade students' mathematics proficiency test performance from 2019 to 2022. These two declines represent the largest drop in student mathematics proficiency in the history of this exam.

- A record number of students scored in the lowest test performance category, below basic, in both mathematics and reading. This was the poorest aggregated performance on this assessment in the history of the NAEP.

Given these results, I wonder how many school districts are allocating the resources suggested by the Harvard study (Goldhaber et al., 2022) to systemically respond to this real unfinished learning.

It should be apparent that we are in a crisis of major proportions. I deeply empathize with the plight of the public school educator and the struggles of pandemic life and pandemic education. I also ask educators to consider the plight of the student. As adults, we are much more equipped to respond to adverse situations cognitively, emotionally, and practically. We have built this resilience over a lifetime of experience, growth, and development. I cannot honestly assess how I would have responded to an event like COVID-19 when I was a young child. I, like most American children, faced developmentally appropriate stress and anxiety, like when asking a girl out on a date or deciding what outfit to wear to the homecoming dance. Educators need advocates, but so do children. Who will work and lobby for their recovery?

Powerful Distractions

Educating children is challenging but rewarding work. Most educators understand that teaching is laborious, and they chose the profession for the potential benefit to children and society. Teaching has consistently been one of the most respected professions in American society. A study found that 95 percent of Americans view teachers favorably, and 89 percent believe teachers deserve more respect (Doonan & Kenneally, 2022). Most members of society know that schools are important and that educators are valuable, but many might not be cognizant of how realities that exist outside of school affect schools and educators. These distractions take many forms. The following sections examine two emerging areas of concern: (1) culture wars and (2) curricular policies. These distractions were important variables in school performance before the pandemic, but like the other factors this chapter examines, they have become more significant in their negative impact since March 2020.

CULTURE WARS

One benefit of living in a pluralistic democratic society like the United States is the fact that we have the right to be different, and we can all live in peace and prosperity if we respect each other's differences. The Bill of Rights in the U.S. Constitution restricts the government's ability to favor or oppress people based on any personal or group characteristic. Public schools are an extension of these principles.

In the previous chapter, I cited the Fourteenth Amendment, which promises U.S. citizens *equal protection under the laws*. We addressed challenges to these liberties in the past, like racial segregation, gender discrimination, and exclusion of students with disabilities. I touted the activism of visionaries who successfully defeated past threats to full educational inclusion. We are experiencing another defining moment in history today.

Critical race theory (CRT) is a legal and academic framework that was developed by attorney Derrick Bell and is widely used in academic papers, policy, and legal decisions that are related to race (Ladson-Billings & Tate, 1995). In 2021, Jelani Cobb, a contributor to *The New Yorker* magazine, wrote an article about Bell and the attention his theory has garnered. Cobb (2021) notes that after years of doing civil rights work as an attorney and seeing limited impact on the lives of ethnic minorities in America:

Bell spent the second half of his career as an academic and, over time, he came to recognize that other decisions in landmark civil-rights cases were of limited practical impact. He drew an unsettling conclusion: racism is so deeply rooted in the makeup of American society that it has been able to reassert itself after each successive wave of reform aimed at eliminating it. Racism, he began to argue, is permanent.

Cobb (2021) writes that CRT is one of a long list of critical frameworks developed to guide critiques of society and policy, like feminist theory, which aims to understand inequality in the area of gender; Marxist theory, used to analyze economic fairness in policy and systems; and Freudian theory, used to examine deeply held psychological motivations inherent in policy and systems.

Bell's theory went relatively unknown among the American public for more than thirty years; that changed with Executive Order 13950, signed by President Donald Trump on September 22, 2020. This order banned institutions that receive federal funding (including public schools) from using training or instructional materials that teach "divisive concepts" (Fix, 2021). Two components of this executive order brought CRT to the forefront of school controversy; a government agency would be in violation of the "divisive concepts" clause if someone felt as though they were being forced into an experience or training that teaches the following.

1. An individual, by virtue of their race or sex, bears responsibility for actions committed in the past by members of the same race or sex.

2. An individual should feel discomfort, guilt, anguish, or another form of psychological distress on account of their race or sex.

The ambiguity of these two provisions set off a political firestorm in state legislatures and school boards across the United States. These provisions didn't provide any guidance on how to objectively assess emotions like guilt or discomfort. By nature, these human emotions are subjective and situational. How could a teacher regulate a student's emotional reaction to a topic or subject presented as part of the curriculum and rooted in historical fact? President Joe Biden revoked Executive Order 13950 in January 2021 (Spiggle, 2021), but the debate about these topics continues.

Stephen Sawchuk (2021), assistant managing editor of *Education Week*, writes that:

Academic understanding of critical race theory differs from representation in recent popular books and, especially, from

> its portrayal by critics. . . . Critics charge that the theory leads
> to negative dynamics, such as a focus on group identity over
> universal, shared traits; divides people into "oppressed" and
> "oppressor" groups; and urges intolerance.

Sawchuk (2021) goes on to assert that the version of CRT expressed by the general public vastly differs from the framework developed by Derrick Bell and that most Americans cannot clearly define the meaning of CRT; the term is often conflated with terms like *antiracism* and *social justice*. One study found that over 70 percent of American citizens can't accurately define or explain critical race theory, and that the framework is almost never taught in K–12 public schools (Safarpour et al., 2021).

The popular and academic versions of CRT have caused legislatures across the United States to propose or adopt legislation that they thought would satisfy Executive Order 13950, even though the order was canceled in January 2021. By the end of 2021, forty-four U.S. states had proposed or passed legislation banning CRT in schools (Schwartz, 2021a). In May 2021, the state of Tennessee passed an anti-CRT law that bans schools from teaching lessons or exposing students to content that causes "discomfort" or "resentment" (Waxman, 2022). This law allows a student, parent, or school employee to file a complaint against a teacher or school district if they have been a victim of the violation of this law. If the teacher or school district is found to be in violation, the complainant can receive compensation equaling 2 percent of the state funding of the violating school system, or $1 million per incident, whichever amount is less. In 2022, a similar anti-CRT law in Oklahoma caused the state board of education to downgrade the accreditation status of Tulsa Public Schools because a district employee attending training on cultural sensitivity and diversity felt shamed by the training (Bikales, 2022). In Florida, a law known as the Stop WOKE Act led the state to reject 54 of 132 previously approved state mathematics textbooks (Atterbury, 2022) and to ban teaching the Advanced Placement African American Studies course (Pitofsky, 2023). In Bozeman, Montana, the debate got so heated that after approving a strategic equity plan aimed at closing some of the district's achievement disparities, citizens responded by attending the next board meeting in protest. The protest produced enough political leverage that the board voted to remove the term *equity* from the district plan and all other district-approved material (Weber, 2021).

These types of policies are having a real, tangible effect on classroom teachers as well. In August 2021, a teacher approached me after I conducted a teacher workshop. His local school board had passed an anti-CRT provision, and he thought he understood the parameters and was willing to comply, though he morally and theoretically disagreed with the policy. He asked if I could give him some advice regarding an incident he found himself currently involved in. As a high school history teacher, he traditionally started the school year by teaching a lesson that was an analysis of the Declaration of Independence, signed on July 4, 1776. He felt that this lesson was appropriate because the start of school in August was chronologically adjacent to the celebration of American Independence Day in July. Historically, he had always included a speech written by abolitionist Frederick Douglass titled "What to the Slave Is the Fourth of July?" This speech is a counternarrative to the traditional view of American independence because it is written from the perspective of African Americans who were still enslaved on July 4, 1776. He told me that this activity always solicited healthy and wholesome debate among his students (who were typically all White) and fostered his school's goal of deepening critical thinking. After he delivered this lesson in 2021, one of his students, the child of a school district board member, shared this experience with his father and expressed that the lesson made him uncomfortable. As a result, the teacher was cited for violating the district's policy and scheduled to have a hearing before the board of education about the termination of his employment with the school district. I am usually never speechless, but in this moment of my career, I did not have a response to his question and dilemma.

Unfortunately, the experience of this teacher is not an isolated incident. One report found that over 50 percent of educators in states with anti-CRT laws have questioned whether to teach lessons about race, gender, or sexual orientation that they have used in the past, and many have stopped teaching lessons on these subjects altogether (Meckler & Natanson, 2022). Another report found that many states, including Florida, are experiencing an increased exodus of teachers of color since the states passed anti-CRT legislation (Bikales, 2022).

There is real, tangible evidence that cultural representation and student learning are linked. Teacher educator Zaretta Hammond (2015) explains the most important factor in the long history of the American achievement gap for students of color (primarily African American and Latino students) is not race but the fact that their culture and experiences have been excluded from the learning experience. She writes:

> The brain is guided by two interconnected prime directives: minimize threats and maximize well-being. Our culture and experiences within the sociopolitical context program our brain regarding how it interprets what is threatening and what is an opportunity for authentic connection with others. (Hammond, 2015, p. 50)

She also asserts that schools have always been responsive to the cultural experience of White students, but to achieve learning success for all students, the curriculum has to make space for the cultural experiences of all students. Teachers are backing away from sound research due to a fear of being sued or terminated because of laws that are antithetical to the egalitarian purpose of the American public school system.

The debate over race is not a new one in American society. Also taking a prominent place in the modern populist debate are gender identity and sexual orientation. In 2022, the state of Florida adopted HB 1157, or what became known as the "Don't Say Gay" law. According to a 2022 report published by the National Education Association (NEA, 2022), the nation's largest teachers' union, the most troubling aspect of the law for LGBTQ advocates is a provision that states:

> Classroom instruction by school personnel or third parties on sexual orientation or gender identity may not occur in kindergarten through grade 3 or in a manner that is not age-appropriate or developmentally appropriate for students in accordance with state standards.

The law was expanded to include banning this content and discussion of the banned content for all grade levels in April 2023 (Ax, 2023). The NEA cites cases of LGBTQ teachers being unfairly targeted and the emotional shame that could be unfairly shouldered by children of LGBTQ parents. As I cited earlier in this chapter, anxiety and depression for students has drastically increased since the beginning of the COVID-19 pandemic, and the data show that LGBTQ youth are at higher risk of anxiety and depression than their non-LGBTQ peers (YouthTruth Student Survey, 2022). Creating laws that systematically vilify or ban representation of a certain segment of a population is antithetical to claims of equality and freedom. Quentin Wittrock (2023), a constitutional scholar and civil rights attorney, writes, "Racial, gender, religious, and other forms of discrimination are terrible things that go directly against the fundamental principles of equality and freedom." These are topics where true allies of the mission of high levels of learning for *all children* cannot "tinker in the gray."

In order to meet Horace Mann's objective to produce a fair school system that allows all citizens a fair shot at living a quality life, that system would have to be prepared to meet the diverse needs of the entire public, not just one segment. It is ironic that school and school district mission statements frequently express the virtue of *learning for all* but some ban a term like *equity*, the living embodiment of the phrase.

This hypocrisy has been debated over the entire history of American public schooling and is one of the last frontiers to achieving Mann's vision (Schement, 2001).

The contemporary culture wars and the resulting laws are unnecessary distractions from collectively addressing the negative psychological and tangible impacts COVID-19 has had on school systems, teachers, and students. These are self-inflicted wounds. American individuals have the freedom to view CRT or the lifestyle choices of others in any way that they choose; opinions are personal and sacred. But if liberty is one of life's natural rights, then it also must follow that any expression of that liberty doesn't infringe on someone else's right to that same liberty.

The evidence shows that nearly three-quarters of American citizens can't accurately define CRT, and it is almost never taught in school. Given this, is CRT worth fighting about, and is the resulting distraction from learning worth it? Will legislating which lifestyles are acceptable or unacceptable to acknowledge in school help us make up for the unfinished learning resulting from the pandemic? Anything that unnecessarily adds stress, anxiety, and fear for professionals and students already reeling from COVID-19 is not a good thing. We are experiencing mass teacher dissatisfaction, a teacher shortage, student dissatisfaction, and learning loss. The real challenges are plentiful; we should avoid self-imposed obstacles, especially those stimulated by a difference of opinion.

As I stated in the previous chapter, I am seeking allies to join me in fulfilling the mission of achieving high levels of learning for all students. Not only do I believe all students can learn, but I also believe all educators can learn. I encourage you to learn more about the life experiences of your students and their families and ruminate on how you can be a positive force in their lives. I invite you to critically examine the evidence that I have presented in this chapter. If current research-backed findings don't align with your personal ideologies, perhaps examine your resistance to them and consider what actions you can take that will still build bridges in your student and family relationships rather than tear them down. If neither option seems palatable, I suggest doing some deep self-examination and reassessing whether working in the public school system is the right choice for your career path.

It is difficult for educators to feel empowered to fight battles on the political fronts where they have no direct control or impact. These culture wars are fronts where people, of all walks of life, need to involve themselves. Unfortunately, the challenges are not just outside of the school premises; we are experiencing some self-inflicted wounds within our spheres of influence.

CURRICULAR POLICIES: "TEACHING WITH FIDELITY"

Our fight for improvement in education has a long history involving legislation and courtrooms, as argued in the previous chapter. Unfortunately, bad policies don't just develop outside of school; they also develop within school systems themselves. It is more difficult to overcome challenges when they are internally produced because they require self-reflection and self-correction. Reflecting on our decisions can trigger self-doubt and poses a threat to the human ego, making it easier to criticize someone else's decision (Bailey & Rehman, 2022). But, if we want to advance the field of education to unprecedented levels of success, self-examination is necessary. One policy trend worthy of examination involves mandated and scripted curricular policies at the district and school levels.

As the COVID-19 pandemic ravaged American society, the federal and state governments stepped in to provide some relief for citizens and institutions that could not proceed with business as usual because of government-mandated shelter-in-place orders. Schools were no different. Recognizing that schools were suffering, the U.S. government passed a huge school relief package, the Elementary and Secondary School Emergency Relief Fund (ESSER) program, which would provide $190 billion in funding for schools over three phases of implementation (U.S. Department of Education, 2022). Textbook companies and educational corporations have descended on school systems to offer prefabricated pathways to student success in the form of scripted curriculum. One school district in Nebraska has earmarked almost a third of its total ESSER allocations to purchase scripted K–12 curricular material in mathematics and reading (Wagner & Dejka, 2022). I am not personally or professionally opposed to educational corporations providing resources for school districts. In my career, I found many of those resources valuable and essential in my job as a public school educator. I am pleased that the government has earmarked such a large amount of money to support the efforts of American public schools. What causes some concern is how some school districts and school leaders are using these tools.

As a former school leader, I am aware of the pressure that rests on the shoulders of school leaders. The culture of high-stakes testing and public school accountability policies can make school leadership a stressful job. According to the German organizational theorist Max Weber (2019), one of the goals of an organization, and more specifically leaders of an organization, is to *reduce uncertainty*. Weber says that because human beings have free will, their behavior can be unpredictable and produce instability within an organization. A good leader creates conditions that reduce behavioral uncertainty and make organizational outcomes and success more predictable. So if someone provides a leader with a resource using terms like *research based* and *guaranteed*, a leader might be attracted to that resource. The promise of a resource that can increase the likelihood of student academic progress, while reducing the probability of human error, would certainly meet Weber's goal of reducing uncertainty. However, human beings are diverse, and no resource or system can totally predict behavior or outcomes. School improvement is a human endeavor—it is messy. The authors of a report titled *How the World's Best Performing School Systems Come Out on Top* assert that "the quality of an education system cannot exceed the quality of its teachers" (Barber & Mourshed, 2007, p. 4). In essence, real school improvement requires a primary investment in human beings, not a resource.

School leaders want to see their students thrive, which can lead leaders to be hasty or fickle consumers of research, and research itself has been debated. For example, a debate exists over the difference between "hard science" and "soft science." Sociologist of science Steven Shapin (2022) explains this debate as one over the validity of natural science compared to social science—a debate to define what science actually *is*. School research is social science. Shapin notes that both forms, natural and social science, are valuable to advance the discipline of science, but he provides a warning in his analysis: because of the unpredictable nature of human behavior, social scientists can overgeneralize their findings and be more susceptible to abuse than natural scientists. In regard to education research, Southern Methodist University professor of education Ken Springer (2010) warns that all education research is *contextual* and that overgeneralizing results can be dangerous and undermine the validity of the research. Like Weber, Springer notes that there are no guarantees or laws in social science; the best that we can hope to accomplish is to reduce uncertainty and create a higher likelihood of success. We can't guarantee it. There is ample evidence that a promise of guaranteed learning outcomes connected to a particular teaching resource or practice is false and deceptive. Educational researcher Robert Marzano (2009) finds that in order for a curriculum to be truly *guaranteed* and *viable* for every student, teachers must develop both a common understanding of that curriculum and a personal commitment to teach it. In Marzano's analysis, the guarantee made in promising student access to the curriculum is the teacher's commitment to teach it, not the learning outcome.

What has caused me concern in this modern context of education is an observed paradigm shift in focus from building the teacher's capacity to improving student outcomes based on the promise of a resource. This message is being sent through the misuse and misunderstanding of the concept of *program fidelity*. Teachers receive curricular resources from leaders who state that the resources are research based and that student success hinges on teachers' adherence to using those resources in the exact manner the developers prescribe, or "with fidelity." This command places a heavy compliance burden on the shoulders of teachers, who, as already noted, have been struggling with unprecedented levels of anxiety and depression.

I have personally witnessed a massive increase in use of the term *with fidelity* as it relates to educational resources. Thomas Guskey (2017), professor emeritus in the College of Education at the University of Kentucky, writes about the miscommunication associated with the term:

> People often use the same word, but the way they use it conveys a very different meaning. For example, "We need to use this program with fidelity." To some [it] means, "ensure those implementing the program include all critical, defining elements," while to others it means "make sure everyone complies and uses it!" . . . The words we use to describe our work communicate a great deal about our profession. Words that bring people together in collaborative efforts to help students offer many positive implications, while those that push compliance . . . or a different meaning of "fidelity" . . . denote a more negative outlook.

The problem is not the term; it is how the term and concept are being communicated, and how teachers are receiving the message. The evidence shows that teachers are not responding favorably.

Tom Rademacher (2017), the 2014 Minnesota Teacher of the Year, writes about how he and his fellow teachers interpret the term *with fidelity*:

> "With fidelity" are some of the most dangerous words in education. . . . Admitting that schools are messy and students are human and teaching is both creative and artistic would also mean you have to trust teachers and let them have some power.

He explains that he and his colleagues perceive focusing on a resource over the judgment of the professional as disrespectful, shortsighted, expensive, and tone-deaf. There is evidence that though teachers are mandated to strictly follow prefabricated curricular resources "with fidelity," very few teachers fully comply. Teachers report that these resources often aren't engaging, aren't culturally appropriate, or don't provide tools for differentiation (Schwartz, 2022a). Again, this leaves teachers in a position to decide between what they believe is best for their students and what might keep them employed. A better approach would be for leaders to recognize that the teacher is the primary means to improving student learning and that the resource is secondary. Teacher empowerment and judgment and the proper use of curricular supplements or resources can coexist if leaders realize that the teacher is the better investment. Also, mistakes are critical to organizational improvement. In his book *Deep Change Leadership: A Model for Renewing and Strengthening Schools and Districts*, Douglas Reeves (2021) argues that implementation errors are essential components of organizational transformation because of the lessons learned from making those errors that educators can use to improve their craft. They provide a platform for self-reflection and build resilience.

Conclusion

We find ourselves in uncharted waters—facing the aftermath of a pandemic and the psychological and physical toll it has taken on our society. Schools, educators, and students are all in the recovery process from this three-year ordeal. It will take years to fully understand the scope of what happened to us.

Educators are struggling. They are struggling with unprocessed and unresolved anxiety connected to the global pandemic. They are recovering from nearly two years of virtual instruction or mitigated face-to-face instruction that they were never properly prepared to deliver. This has led to record-low teacher morale and record-high teacher resignation. When we couple these realities with historically low numbers of newly credentialed teachers entering our field, and governments passing emergency legislation that puts some of the most unprepared teachers in front of the most vulnerable students, we have a crisis.

Students, who are a lot less emotionally and psychologically developed than adults, are struggling with their own challenges. They were subjected to two years of isolation during the COVID-19 pandemic, and the quality of their experiences hinged greatly on the economic status and stability of their homes. Students found virtual learning difficult and challenging, and many became disengaged; now, we as educators face student learning gaps that will take years to fix. These same students, because of their social isolation, are experiencing higher levels of anxiety and depression, and they find school employees more harmful than helpful in addressing their mental health.

Our society has become completely polarized politically. Culture wars over curricular content have led to laws that allow parents and others to sue teachers and school districts over content that made their children feel discomfort. This has led teachers to feel reluctant to teach culturally responsive content that has been proven to improve student engagement and student learning. It has also made members of the community at large, like LGBTQ students and families, feel as if they are unwanted second-class citizens.

Finally, we are experiencing leaders spending more resources on buying prefabricated curricular models than on investing in the retention and development of their teachers. Like the culture war policies, the modern educator is faced with a set of new mandates—not mandates about controversial topics, but mandates to implement curricular models "with fidelity." This approach does not consider that the best schools in the world invest in people primarily and resources secondarily. Improvement requires errors and self-reflection; however, many modern school leaders are after quick fixes that they hope might improve state test scores, but that instead alienate teachers and don't meet the diverse needs of students.

We find ourselves in quite a quandary. Will we wither under the pressure of our modern challenges, or will we respond like generations of the past by unifying and carving a collective pathway to improvement? In the next chapter, I would like to prove that a full understanding of and commitment to the PLC at Work process will help us navigate these modern challenges and propel our system to new heights.

Pause to Think and Plan

Amen!

Aha!

So What?

CHAPTER 4

The Future — Where Do We Go From Here?

I hope what this book has proven thus far is that the journey of the American public school system has been long and full of challenges and victories with detours and changes in direction. Though bumpy, it has been a journey worth taking. As someone who grew up experiencing the underbelly of the school system by attending racially and socioeconomically segregated schools, I entered the profession with something to prove, a chip on my shoulder. I knew that kids like me, from communities like mine, were highly intelligent, capable, and worth fighting for. In 2001, my mission received its most valuable boost when I attended a Professional Learning Communities at Work conference at Adlai E. Stevenson High School in Lincolnshire, Illinois. Though I was reluctant when I arrived, I left energized, inspired, and focused on making the impact in education that I had always hoped to make. This time, my desire was supported by a framework that would bring it to reality. This experience would change the entire trajectory of my professional career. At the conclusion of this chapter, I am hopeful that a reintroduction of the PLC at Work process will have the same impact on you that it had on me in 2001.

Learning Organizations, Learning Communities, PLCs, and PLCs at Work

The concept of people working together within an organization to achieve a common objective is not new, and it is not new to schools. Many iterations of collaborative models for organizational advancement have been produced over the years. As a brand-new middle school teacher, I was introduced to the middle school team or "house" concept in the early 1990s. The idea was to make middle schools less industrial and create caring communities of teachers who taught different subjects but similar students and met regularly to act as empathetic advocates for students, mainly focused on their adolescent social and emotional needs. This structure of collaboration was a recommendation by the Turning Points Commission, who published their report in 1989 (Carnegie Corporation of New York, 1989). The commission was assembled to study a national crisis in adolescent education and make recommendations for improvement. In the early 1990s, this research was considered cutting edge, and my school organized teachers based on this adolescent support model.

After spending several years as a member of an interdisciplinary team with no real concrete structure, I found that these meetings became emotionally draining and even counterproductive. Instead of strategically collaborating about real student needs, emotional or academic, my teammates spent most of our time venting frustrations about student behavior, administrative decisions, or lack of parental involvement. I found these meetings so emotionally draining that I would often schedule parent meetings or other obligations so that I would have an excuse not to attend. What was the lesson? I learned early on that not all collaboration is valuable; in fact, poor collaboration can be damaging. In 2000, Anthony Jackson and Gayle Davis authored the book *Turning Points 2000: Educating Adolescents in the 21st Century*. This book was a review of more than ten years of implementation of the Turning Points research. Jackson and Davis (2000) found that the loose model of general discussion of student social and emotional needs was inadequate and could undermine positive school culture. They proposed a change to the original collaborative model:

> All the Turning Points principles, taken together, lead toward
> a single goal: ensuring that every student achieves success.
> We define success as the Turning Points vision of a 15-year-old
> who, after a successful experience in the middle grades, is
> intellectually reflective, caring, ethical, healthy, a good citizen,

> and en route to a lifetime of meaningful work. To reach that
> goal, middle grades educators must substantially strengthen
> the heart of schooling—teaching and learning. (Jackson & Davis,
> 2000, p. 63)

I am not claiming that collaborating about student social and emotional needs is unimportant; in fact, given the data presented in chapter 3 (page 43), the evidence would suggest that this is more important than ever. What I am asserting is that any collaborative effort that is not intentional, organized, and outcomes driven will eventually fall apart and potentially become more damaging than beneficial.

LEARNING ORGANIZATIONS

In 1990, Peter Senge, a systems scientist and senior lecturer at the Massachusetts Institute of Technology, published a book that would be considered one of the most influential works of the 20th century: *The Fifth Discipline: The Art and Practice of the Learning Organization*. This book would make a critical impact on Richard DuFour and Robert Eaker and what later became known as Professional Learning Communities at Work.

Senge (1990) asserts that learning organizations have five disciplines.

1. **Personal mastery:** The development of the individual

2. **Mental models:** Deeply ingrained assumptions that shape how we view reality

3. **Shared vision:** The unearthing of shared pictures of the organization's future

4. **Team learning:** The capacity of a team to suspend assumptions and think together

5. **Systems thinking:** A focus on the whole instead of individual parts

Senge asserts that the fifth discipline, *systems thinking*, is the discipline that binds the learning organization together.

Schools are organized for individual practice. Teachers are separated into classrooms, and students learn within the four walls of the teacher's autonomous domain. Almost everything about the traditional school system is individually focused. The teacher is responsible for their individual grade level or subject matter, learning objectives, lesson planning and delivery, classroom management, and student evaluation systems. In fact, schools evaluate each teacher individually on these responsibilities. The student is also looked at through the lens of individuality; their success or failure lies solely in their individual performance both academically and behaviorally. Schools, in essence, have been an archipelago—a collection of individual islands. Senge's vision of systems thinking, the fifth discipline, challenges members of an institution to shift their focus from individual success to collective success. Our history and structure in schools make this challenge even more difficult for us than for other organizations.

LEARNING COMMUNITIES

After the introduction of learning organizations and systems thinking by Peter Senge (1990), a whole body of literature started to emerge. An important addition to the foundation laid by Senge was championed by Thomas Sergiovanni, professor of education and administration at Trinity University. Sergiovanni (1994) felt it was essential that the description of the organization's collaboration be more personal, more familial. He championed changing the description from learning *organization* to learning *community*. He felt the term *community* created the type of bond that schools needed to improve their collective impact. He argued that organizations, no matter how successful, are more concerned with promoting individual success than making a moral and community impact, which is a principle at the heart of school success.

In a paper presented in 1993 at the annual meeting of the American Educational Research Association in Atlanta, Georgia, which predates his popular journal article published in 1994, Sergiovanni (1993) asserts the following:

> Not all groupings of individuals . . . can be characterized as organizations. Families, communities, friendship networks and social clubs are examples of collections of people that are different. And because of these differences the practices that make sense in schools understood as organizations just don't fit. (p. 6)
>
> Communities are socially organized around relationships and the felt interdependencies that nurture them. (p. 7)

Sergiovanni felt that schools are much too complex to be considered just organizations. In order to be truly successful, they would need to tap into a level of connection more profound than individual success; they would need to have a passion for morally driven collective success. Thus, the term *learning communities* started to replace the term *learning organizations* in schools.

PROFESSIONAL LEARNING COMMUNITIES

After Sergiovanni's input, a new term started to circulate in educational circles. That term was *professional learning community (PLC)*. In the 1993 book *Teachers' Work: Individuals, Colleagues, and Contexts*, Judith Warren Little and Milbrey Wallin McLaughlin introduced the benefits of having teachers work collaboratively to improve professional practice through a structure called *professional learning communities*. They asserted that professional practice was more likely to improve, and improve drastically, if teachers belonged to a collective unit that allowed them to address issues of practice together.

Shirley Hord, another early advocate for this term and concept, described a PLC in the following terms in a 1997 article: "an organizational arrangement, the professional learning community is seen as a powerful staff development approach and a potent strategy for school change and improvement." Hord (1997) asserted that PLCs have five essential elements.

1. Supportive and shared leadership

2. Collective creativity

3. Shared values and vision

4. Supportive conditions

5. Shared personal practice

This contribution to the concept of learning communities was important because of the addition of professional practice. Sergiovanni's (1993) concern about interconnectedness and shared community was an important contribution to advocate for interdependence, but many, like Hord (1997), saw the community as more than a tight-knit network of individuals who shared a common bond; they saw that it had the potential to drastically improve teacher practice (DuFour & DuFour, 2006).

The history of the PLC movement is an interesting one. Understanding the evolution of this movement will help educators apply PLC principles in the modern context. Solution Tree, the publisher of this book, offers a wonderful two-part documentary on this history on the AllThingsPLC website (www.allthingsplc.info/Origins-of-PLCs). This insightful documentary is a resource for anyone who wants to understand the history of the PLC movement at a deeper level.

PROFESSIONAL LEARNING COMMUNITIES AT WORK

In 1998, two longtime friends, Richard DuFour and Robert Eaker, authored the book *Professional Learning Communities at Work: Best Practices for Enhancing Student Achievement*. This book was the foundation for my great enlightenment in the Adlai E. Stevenson High School auditorium in 2001, and it will be the foundation for this book from this point forward.

Richard DuFour was a career practitioner. He served as a teacher, principal, and superintendent, eventually retiring from public education after more than thirty years of service. Robert Eaker spent most of his career as an academic. He served as a long-time professor of education, dean, and provost at Middle Tennessee State University in Murfreesboro, Tennessee. DuFour and Eaker were fans and students of the scholars and scholarship cited in the previous sections. Later, the duo would be joined by Rebecca DuFour, a former elementary teacher and the wife of Richard DuFour. The trio would form an amazing team that would spend the next twenty years advancing the work together. The team, often called the "Three Rs," eventually added Mike Mattos, a leading thought leader in student interventions and support (response to intervention [RTI]), as a fourth member. Unfortunately, the team would lose the contributions of Richard DuFour and Rebecca DuFour when they passed away in 2017 and 2018, respectively.

DuFour and Eaker were frank in their admission that they did not create the term *professional learning community*; what they created was the framework that would guide and enhance a school's ability to implement and live the goals of a professional learning community. In *A Summing Up: Teaching and Learning in Effective Schools and PLCs at Work*, Eaker (2020) writes about the motivation for creating the PLC at Work framework with DuFour:

> What we did do, I think, is use our experience and backgrounds to develop a framework for describing what occurs in a high-performing school that functions as a professional learning community—day in and day out. And we set out to describe, in detail, the practices and processes school leaders could utilize to transform more traditional school cultures into high-performing professional learning communities. This is why we added the *at work* designation to the term *professional learning community*. For us, the phrase *at work* would be the central focus of our

new book about schools that function as professional learning
communities and our future efforts to improve schools. (p. 133)

This framework resonated with educators across the world. Since 1998, when DuFour and Eaker's seminal work was published, over 150 additional books based on the tenets of that original work have been published. The demand for the concepts DuFour and Eaker developed became so great that they had to deputize practitioners. These practitioners, who would come to be called *PLC associates*, had to produce evidence of their school's or district's effective implementation of the PLC at Work process to be eligible to provide training for the thousands of schools and school districts that wanted to learn more about the process. I became a PLC associate in 2003. As of 2023, there are over 350 PLC associates. In addition to the books and associates, there have been articles, school-based workshops, local and national conferences, international conferences, coaching, and recorded and streaming videos made available to educators all over the world in support of the PLC at Work process. Only a few educational innovations have sustained this type of continuous growth over a twenty-five-year period.

So what are Professional Learning Communities at Work? A *PLC at Work* is defined as "an ongoing process in which educators work collaboratively in recurring cycles of collective inquiry and action research to achieve better results for the students they serve" (DuFour, DuFour, Eaker, Many, & Mattos, 2016, p. 10). From this point forward, when I use the terms *PLC* and *PLC at Work* in this book, I am explicitly referring to this definition.

The purpose of this book is not to summarize and restate twenty-five years of work done within the PLC at Work movement. As I described previously, there are ample resources and opportunities available for anyone who wants to gain a deeper understanding of the concepts. My purpose is to reintroduce the concepts in light of the aftermath of the global COVID-19 pandemic and to help schools re-examine their understanding of and commitment to the PLC at Work process. Perhaps it is the most appropriate tool to guide us out of the dark space we currently inhabit. In addition, I have become troubled by the chronic misunderstanding of PLC at Work and poor implementation of the concepts since 1998. I have observed that over the past twenty-five years, as the PLC at Work process has become more universally known and embraced (at least at a surface level), educators have started to water down the concepts to fit their personal and collective comfort levels. This concept—*PLC Lite*—is described in chapter 1 (page 11).

What I have often observed as I have worked directly with schools since 2003 is not a reflection of DuFour and Eaker's PLC at Work framework, but something much less comprehensive and impactful. The softening of an innovation is not new in education. Mary Kennedy (2005), professor emeritus in the Department of Teacher Education at Michigan State University, finds that it is common for the realities and intentions of researchers to be different from the realities and intentions of practitioners in the implementation of a new concept. Researchers tend to develop innovations based on a reality that is falsely utopian, and educators have to implement those innovations in an environment that is usually messier and more unpredictable than their architects envisioned. As a result of these mismatched realities, innovations rarely get implemented the way that they were originally intended (Kennedy, 2005).

In an article he wrote in 2004, Richard DuFour shared his personal observation of the disconnect emerging between the PLC at Work research and practical application in schools:

> The idea of improving schools by developing professional learning communities is currently in vogue. People use this term to describe every imaginable combination of individuals with an interest in education—a grade-level teaching team, a school committee, a high school department, an entire school district, a state department of education, a national professional organization, and so on. In fact, the term has been used so ubiquitously that it is in danger of losing all meaning.

I do not want PLC at Work to end up as an artifact in the museum of failed educational change, just another abbreviation placed alongside other forgotten innovations. Our past and present dictate that the future calls for more substance—something more sustainable. The stakes and the obstacles are enormous; the response to these challenges has to be equally enormous.

The casual use of the abbreviation *PLC* that DuFour describes has been frustrating. My fellow PLC associates and I have tried to impress upon teachers and school leaders that associating the term *PLC* with any loose or unstructured gathering of educators can undermine the potential potency of the practice. The title *at Work* is what makes the gathering of educators come to life and produce a powerful impact on student learning. Educators might refer to a gathering of educators as "a PLC"; although that is not an accurate use of the term, I am less concerned about what a fellow educator calls the team or the meeting than I am deeply concerned about the clarity of and commitment to the *work* that team will engage in.

THE NEED FOR A MOVEMENT

Why are people reluctant to fully commit to a revolutionary idea? I have always found it puzzling how many people hear about, agree on, and applaud the PLC at Work process but very few fully engage in it. Change is challenging, especially essential shifts in habits. At the core of the PLC at Work process is the need to critically change traditions, especially those traditions and practices that are destructive to the goal of high levels of learning for all students.

In 1951, moral and social philosopher Eric Hoffer authored the classic book *The True Believer: Thoughts on the Nature of Mass Movements*. In the book, Hoffer analyzes history and parses the nature of critical social movements of the past. He finds that social movements contain three essential elements that resonate with the masses and spark a collective rejection of the status quo (Hoffer, 1951).

1. Complete dissatisfaction with the status quo (urgency)

2. An idea worth personal sacrifice (passion)

3. A sense of power (efficacy)

Dissatisfaction is the catalyst to change; satisfied people do not change. Change can be such a disruptive and inconvenient process that people tend to make a pragmatic decision before voluntarily deciding to confront an uncomfortable reality. Is the inconvenience of change worth the potential improvement or benefit? According to Hoffer (1951), if the answer is no, then the current reality is worth tolerating and people become what he calls *conscious accommodators*. These are people who are miserable but content.

An argument for complacency in the field of education is the personal experience of the traditional educator. Scholar and teacher Dan Lortie published the seminal work *Schoolteacher: A Sociological Study* in 1975. In this book, he theorizes that change and self-reflection in the field of education are challenging because of two experiences. He calls these experiences the *apprenticeship of observation* and finds them to be unique to the field of education (Lortie, 1975).

1. Educators have been socialized within their field of practice since kindergarten (four to five years old).

2. Most educators experienced success and validation within the traditional system.

According to Lortie (1975), the positive socialization of most educators within the traditional system causes them to view the system as *perfect* and the struggling student as *defective*. He points out that educators who struggled within the traditional system are more empathetic toward struggling students and are generally more willing to participate in change. Could these experiences explain some of the general apathy toward student failure we face today?

In 2014, Robert Marzano and his associates (Marzano, Warrick, & Simms, 2014) introduced to the field of education a systemic response to education's general apathy toward student failure. They called this approach High Reliability Schools. Marzano and his associates argue that student learning is so important, and the consequences of failure so high, that schools should intentionally, methodically, and systemically monitor all the critical indicators of student learning like a nuclear plant operator works to prevent nuclear meltdown. They state:

> "In industries where mistakes and errors lead to significant and far-reaching consequences—such as nuclear power plants, air traffic control towers, and electrical power grids—organizations must adjust their operations to proactively prevent failure. . . . A high reliability school, by definition, monitors the effectiveness of critical factors within the system and immediately takes action to contain the negative effects of any errors that occur." (Marzano et al., 2014, p. 1)

Student education is high stakes, and the consequences of failure are dire. So how could educators be aware of this fact and not be grossly dissatisfied and moved to swift collective action? Schools have long engaged in the rhetoric of egalitarianism. Our mission statements are full of declarations about concern for "all students," yet the reality has never lived up to the theory:

> The hypocritical need of school systems and our society to portray egalitarianism, while behaving like a meritocracy, creates an environment of comfort and stagnation. Until there is a thorough examination of the nature of this hypocrisy, equality will never be a reality in schools; it will only be a buzzword used to tickle the ears. (Muhammad, 2015, p. 41)

If we are truly going to make substantive improvements to student learning in the field of education, we need a movement. Conscious accommodation and casual observation of student failure will not produce the urgency, passion, and efficacy necessary to make the future brighter than the past. Change presents a lot of challenges, but the inconvenience and discomfort we experience are both worthwhile when they are for a noble cause. I cannot think of anything nobler than securing a bright future for a child. I cannot think of a nobler profession than the field of education. We can no longer wait for people on the outside to guide our change; a revolution of concern has to develop from within. The PLC at Work model provides us with a road map to that revolution. When that revolution takes place, our community, our nation, and our world become better places. I believe that when properly implemented, the PLC at Work process can be the most powerful and sustainable education movement in the history of public education.

For the remainder of this chapter, my goal is to reintroduce the reader to the theoretical premise of the PLC at Work process: the three big ideas. I aim to provide a pathway for successfully creating a system that can apply the philosophical foundation of the process: the six characteristics of a PLC. I will conclude the chapter with a challenge to the reader to become reeducated on the process and recommit to implementing the process fully and successfully.

Paradigm Shift: The Three Big Ideas of a PLC at Work

As I sat waiting for the PLC at Work conference to begin in 2001, I had no intention of engaging intellectually or emotionally. I was a reluctant participant. But the ideas and concepts the architects of PLC at Work presented were so intriguing and relevant that I experienced a major life event—a paradigm shift. Merriam-Webster defines a *paradigm shift* as "an important change that happens when the usual way of thinking about or doing something is replaced by a new and different way" (Paradigm shift, n.d.). What I experienced could also be referred to as an *epiphany*: "a usually sudden manifestation or perception of the essential nature or meaning of something" (Epiphany, n.d.). This experience forever changed me as an educator. This shift in perception reshaped my ideas about the fundamental purpose of schooling, school structure, teaching practices, curriculum, and leadership. Almost everything that I've done since as a practitioner, author, and consultant has been shaped by that experience.

The paradigm shift I experienced was the effect of being introduced to and understanding the three big ideas (DuFour et al., 2016) that drive the PLC at Work process.

1. A focus on learning

2. A collaborative culture and collective responsibility

3. A results orientation

"The progress a district or school experiences on the PLC journey will be largely dependent on the extent to which these ideas are considered, understood, and ultimately embraced by its members" (DuFour et al., 2016, p. 11).

I suggest that a re-examination of these three concepts could stimulate an epiphany and a renewed commitment to the PLC at Work process, even if you have considered them in the past. The current context of education, including those psychological and tangible effects brought about by the COVID-19 pandemic, may cause you to rethink the relevance and importance of these concepts that have been around since 1998.

BIG IDEA ONE: A FOCUS ON LEARNING

My greatest experience in my professional awakening at Adlai E. Stevenson High School was deep reflection on the first big idea: a focus on learning. At first consideration, this idea doesn't seem so big. It appears to be blatantly obvious. Of course a school should focus on learning. What was so critical in my paradigm shift was my experience as a teacher—what I had experienced to that point in my career. Rarely had my school's system or practices truly focused on student learning. We were more concerned about student compliance and monitoring the process of education than measurable learning.

In 1970, Martin Haberman and Dale Brubaker introduced a concept to the education research community called *schoolsmanship*. They argued that schools are not truly organized around intentional academic outcomes, but rather are organized to create conditions that make students more amenable to schooling, therefore emphasizing behaviors like compliance, timeliness, and background knowledge. Learning, they argued, is a secondary priority. Students receive positive feedback from the system (for example, perfect-attendance and citizenship awards) if they comply with the conditions of schoolsmanship, even if they have learned very little. Haberman and Brubaker (1970) did not argue that characteristics of schoolsmanship, like timeliness, are unimportant to a student's development. Instead, they argued that learning is not the school's top priority—socialization and compliance are (Haberman & Brubaker, 1970). The Coleman Report of 1966 (Coleman et al., 1966), tasked with assessing U.S. schools' impact on student progress at the time, reached a similar conclusion. Schools were doing little to advance students intellectually, especially students who were ethnic minorities or poor (Dickinson, 2016). The depressing conclusion the Coleman Report reached was that student learning and intellect are more influenced by the home environment, and schools have little influence over closing the home support gap. This conclusion has been successfully challenged by many dedicated researchers since it was published (Petrides & Nodine, 2005). We know that schools can compensate for home and socialization factors, but many educators still echo the sentiments of the Coleman Report decades later.

The first big idea of the PLC at Work process asserts that schools can make a huge impact on students' intellectual growth when educators collectively focus on the important activities that students experience at school. What the student learns—what they tangibly take away from the experience—is what is most important. The process is negotiable, but the outcome is not. If a school focuses on this essential principle, and embraces the practices that support this principle, more students will learn at high levels. Hattie (2009) writes about this concept in *Visible Learning: A Synthesis of Over 800 Meta-Analyses Related to Achievement*:

> The act of teaching requires deliberate interventions to ensure that there is cognitive change in the student: thus the key ingredients are awareness of the learning intentions, knowing when a student is successful in attaining those intentions, having sufficient understanding of the student's understanding as [they come] to the task, and knowing enough about the content to provide meaningful and challenging experiences in some sort of progressive development. It involves an experienced teacher who knows a range of learning strategies to provide the students when they seem *not* to understand. (p. 23)

The first big idea in the PLC at Work process posits that in order to achieve those conditions that improve student learning, schools need to organize teachers into collaborative teams and act in the following manner to clarify the answers to the following questions:

- **What is it we want our students to know?** What knowledge, skills, and dispositions must all students acquire as a result of this grade level, this course, and this unit we are about to teach? What systems have we put in place to ensure we are providing every student with access to a guaranteed and viable curriculum regardless of the teacher to whom that student might be assigned?

- **How will we know if our students are learning?** How can we check for understanding on an ongoing basis in our individual classrooms? How will we gather evidence of each student's proficiency as a team? What criteria will we establish to assess the quality of student work? How can we be certain we can apply the criteria consistently?

- **How will we respond when students do not learn?** What steps can we put in place to provide students who struggle with additional time and support for learning in a way that is timely, directive, and systematic rather than invitational and random? How can we provide students with multiple opportunities to demonstrate mastery?

- **How will we enrich and extend the learning for students who are proficient?** How can we differentiate instruction among us so that the needs of all students are being met without relying on rigid tracking? (DuFour & Marzano, 2011, pp. 22–23, emphasis added)

The four bolded questions are often referred to as the *four critical questions* of the PLC at Work process. These four questions guide the work of a system truly focused on learning. What struck me so deeply and caused my epiphany at the conference in 2001 was not just the concept of learning as a school's primary focus but the coordinated process that would engage teachers in a critical set of practices proven to increase the probability of student learning. I could not wait to leave that conference and go back and organize my school in this fashion. To help me truly comprehend the interdependence of the four critical questions, I developed some synonyms that simplified the process so that I could better communicate it to assist with implementation.

- **Target:** Question one asks, Learn what?
- **Evidence:** Question two asks, How will we know?
- **Action:** Question three asks, What will we do if they don't learn?
- **Action:** Question four asks, What will we do if they do learn?

Teachers concerned about student learning would collaboratively agree on a specific *target*, the destination of the student's learning journey. Teachers collaboratively engaged in creating and analyzing formative assessments would gather *evidence* of the student's current proximity to the target. Teachers collaboratively engaged in responding to the evidence of student learning would take *action* to support or extend each student's learning based on the evidence they gathered. This simplification of the four critical questions helped me and my teachers successfully translate this information from theory to action. The questions were a professional compass at the center of all our professional behaviors—simple, but powerful. I would like to prove that the critical shift answering the four questions creates can have the same effect on your learning environment.

Critical Question One: What is it we want our students to know?

If learning, the actual acquisition of essential knowledge and skills, is the primary purpose of a school, then someone has to determine what students need to learn. As we examined in the previous chapter, populist politics and narrow views of culture are not good influences in determining what all students should learn. We also discovered that leaving this job to multinational educational corporations alone won't lead to the type of deep curricular experience that our students deserve. So who is best qualified to answer this critical question? The teachers who instruct students daily are. I will establish with big idea two (a collaborative culture) that this task is best completed collectively as opposed to individually. So what work do teachers need to engage in to answer the question, Learn what?

There are a few important facts that will enhance teachers' focus on the objective of PLC critical question one and enhance their collective proficiency. W. James Popham (2021), professor emeritus of education at the University of California, Los Angeles, asserts that because the potential subjects and topics of classroom instruction are vast, we need some local and national consensus about what is absolutely important for students to learn in order to improve school reliability. I would argue that this alignment should go beyond the local and state levels, and there should be reliability from classroom to classroom in every individual school. The second critical conclusion that will help teams with this task is the painful realization we have too many standards and not all standards are equally important (Lawrence, Loi, & Gudex, 2019). Schools need a protocol to emphasize the most important learning outcomes over less important standards. Teaching is challenging enough without the added burden of teaching things that are not critically important.

Before teacher teams deeply engage in collaboration to answer this first critical question, they need some common vocabulary to guide their work as defined by the Glossary of Education Reform (www.edglossary.org).

- **Learning standard:** "Learning standards are concise, written descriptions of what students are expected to know and be able to do at a specific stage of their education. Learning standards describe educational objectives—i.e., what students should have learned by the end of a course, grade level, or grade span—but they do not describe any particular teaching practice" (Learning standards, 2014).

- **Curriculum:** "The term *curriculum* refers to the lessons and academic content taught in a school or in a specific course or program" (Curriculum, 2015).

Teacher teams should gather essential documents and engage in collaborative study about what content is absolutely essential for every student enrolled in their courses to learn. Some of the documents a team might consider include:

- Current state or provincial standards
- Recommended standards from professional organizations
- District curriculum guides
- A list of prerequisite skills that colleagues at the next course or grade level have established as essential for success at the level
- Assessment frameworks (how students will be assessed on state, provincial, and other district and national assessments)
- Data on student performance on past assessments
- Examples of student work and specific criteria that could be tested in judging the quality of student work
- Recommendations and standards for workplace skills (for example, industry standards for career and technical education programs)
- Recommendations on standards and curriculum design from [established authors and thought leaders] (DuFour, DuFour, Eaker, Mattos, & Muhammad, 2021, pp. 155–156)

I would like to add a tenth resource to the preceding list:

- A list of social and emotional standards, along with longitudinal data on nonacademic student needs (like discipline and attendance data) given the enormous increase in student psychological and emotional suffering after the COVID-19 pandemic

The ideal product of this collaborative effort is best described by Marzano (2003) as a *guaranteed and viable curriculum*. Marzano (2003) asserts a curriculum meets these criteria when (1) it gives students access to the same essential learning regardless of who is teaching the class and (2) it can be taught within the time allotted for instruction. A team of teachers can meet this standard when they:

- Study the intended curriculum [together]

- Agree on priorities within the curriculum

- Clarify how the curriculum translates into student knowledge and skills

- Establish general pacing guidelines for delivering the curriculum

- Commit to one another that they will, in fact, teach the agree-upon curriculum (DuFour & Marzano, 2011, p. 91)

Engaging in the process of producing a guaranteed and viable curriculum can have a positive effect on teachers and students. It can promote clear and consistent learning priorities for both teachers and students, and clearer and more effective formative assessments. It can establish reasonable and viable learning goals for every student to achieve, and create a sense of community and personal ownership among those who agree to teach the curriculum (DuFour, DuFour, & Eaker, 2008).

Critical Question Two: How will we know if our students are learning?

The PLC at Work process posits that once a team of teachers can agree on what every student must know and be able to do and they can create a guaranteed and viable curriculum, that team needs to determine what success in that curriculum will look like. The team members also need to agree about the tools used to gather evidence of learning. That evidence then determines the effectiveness or ineffectiveness of the strategies the teacher or team used in their attempt to deliver proficiency on important learning objectives. This activity is so sacred that Richard DuFour (2015) defined it as the lynchpin of the PLC at Work process. It is the practice that holds all the pieces together.

Assessment practices in education have historically hindered the cause of student learning more than promoted learning. Many assessments, such as IQ tests, standardized state or national assessments, and even teacher-generated classroom assessments, have been focused more on sorting students into categories of aptitude than on incrementally improving the comprehension of all students (Sparks, 1999). As a teacher, I can remember my own assessment practices, and I am ashamed to admit that they did little to improve my students' comprehension. My school's culture allowed me and my colleagues to assess student mastery in any format we chose and to use (or not use) the evidence gained from those assessments autonomously as well. This led us to solely use our assessment practices to identify who *met* our success criteria and who *did not meet* those criteria. I noticed over the course of a semester or a school year that the feedback I was giving students about their learning was not improving their comprehension, confidence, or engagement. So why did I keep giving it? Thomas Guskey (2015) identifies three reasons why we are reluctant to examine our traditional assessment practices, and they are more social and cultural than professional.

1.   Grades have historically been the most important criteria in determining a student's success in school, and changing assessment practices might negatively impact student motivation, attendance, engagement, and compliance to systemic requirements.

2.   Schools have traditionally been organized to sort students we deem more intelligent from those who are less intelligent; traditional grading and assessment practices help sustain the traditional system.

3.   Schools feed graduates into a society that is hierarchical, and traditional grading and assessment practices help students recognize who is qualified for specific roles in our society. Students with good grades pursue vocations that require thinking and high intelligence. Students with poor grades pursue vocations that require manual labor or less cognitive ability.

So if we are going to work toward the goal of high levels of learning for all students, these assumptions and the practices that they produce have to be challenged and reformed.

In order for assessments to be critical tools in advancing student learning, we need to use them formatively. Rick Stiggins (2002), a pioneer in the advancement of effective assessment practices, has helped educators clearly distinguish between assessment practices that advance the mission of improving student learning and those that do not. Stiggins (2002) clarifies that a *summative assessment* is an assessment *of* learning, a tool used to clarify whether the student learned or did not learn an objective within a given period of time. He compares this assessment practice to that of formative assessment. A *formative assessment* is intended to be an assessment *for* learning, a tool used to inform both the teacher and the student about the student's current level of achievement. This practice can guide the teacher's future instruction, help the student understand what steps they must take to further their learning, and motivate the student to take those steps. The PLC at Work process depends on teachers' using formative assessments collaboratively.

As with critical question one, teams can benefit from agreeing on some common vocabulary as defined by the Glossary of Education Reform (www.edglossary.org).

- **Assessment:** "The wide variety of methods or tools that educators use to evaluate, measure, and document the academic readiness, learning progress, skill acquisition, or educational needs of students" (Assessment, 2015)

- **Summative assessment:** Tools "used to evaluate student learning, skill acquisition, and academic achievement at the conclusion of a defined instructional period—typically at the end of a project, unit, course, semester, program, or school year" (Summative assessment, 2013)

- **Formative assessment:** Tools "used to identify individual student weaknesses and strengths so that educators can provide specialized academic support, educational programming, or social services" (Assessment, 2015)

- **Criterion-referenced assessment:** Tests or assessments "designed to measure student performance against a fixed set of predetermined criteria or learning standards—i.e., concise, written descriptions of what students are expected to know and be able to do at a specific stage of their education" (Criterion-referenced test, 2014)

If teacher teams were organized to use assessment practices that actually improve student learning instead of just measure student learning, they would act in the following manner (Bailey & Jakicic, 2023).

1. Decide what to assess.

2. Decide how to assess.

3. Develop the assessment plan.

4. Determine the timeline.

5. Write the assessment.

6. Review the assessment before administration.

7. Set proficiency criteria and decide how to gather the data.

In their book *Common Formative Assessment: A Toolkit for Professional Learning Communities at Work*, Kim Bailey and Chris Jakicic (2023) provide many more important nuances that would promote success in the assessment framework they designed. But I hope it is clear that if collaborative teams engaged in the work these authors suggest, we could advance our mission to achieve high levels of learning for all students.

The benefits associated with collaboratively developing assessments and using the evidence in a formative manner are abundant. Paul Black and Dylan Wiliam (1998), after conducting a meta-analysis of over 250 studies on formative assessments, found that assessments used formatively are tremendously likely to greatly accelerate student learning. In 2008, Dylan Wiliam and Marnie Thompson found that collaboratively creating common formative assessments can facilitate outstanding benefits in student learning compared to having individual teachers take on this task alone. Those benefits include the following.

- Strong content expertise is critical to creating powerful assessments, and a collaborative team of teachers are likely to possess deeper content knowledge collectively than any one teacher has individually.

- Collaboratively created common formative assessments provide a powerful form of action research. The results gathered on the team's assessments are from the teachers' students, not students they are unfamiliar with or students who are different from their own.

- The sense of community felt on a strong collaborative team helps teachers persevere through the discomfort of receiving feedback on their instruction and allows them to stay more engaged in the process.

- Creating, implementing, and learning from the results of team-developed assessments brings about powerful and organic professional learning.

- Formative assessments commonly developed, implemented, and utilized by a team of teachers help teachers transition more quickly from a focus on teaching to a focus on learning.

Critical Question Three: How will we respond when students do not learn?

Anyone who has ever taught knows that students learn in different ways and at different paces. So if classrooms are structured in a fixed manner where all students are typically taught the same way for a common amount of time, some students might learn an objective in the time allotted, while others might not. If a school is truly concerned about student learning, it should produce an accessible systematic response to students who fail to meet an essential learning outcome in the time allotted for that task. The answers to questions one and two make clear what the student is expected to learn and the way that learning is to be assessed. What is still unclear is how the team, and the school in general, will respond when students don't learn.

Historically, schools have not responded systematically when students have fallen short of learning expectations. Instead, many practitioners have relied on the punitive effects of a negative grade or unfavorable feedback to improve students' school commitment and performance. In many cases, educators have defended these practices under the premise that the negative feedback is for the good of the student. Assessment expert Tom Schimmer (2023) notes:

> The penalties are "for their own good" and "important life lessons." While preparation for life after school is a noble cause, admonitions such as, "Wait until you enter the real world" disrespect and dismiss students. Adults in schools tend to draw a fictional line between the student world and the adult world. (p. 1)

This approach to shaping student improvement is normal, though it has been ineffective. B. F. Skinner, an influential 20th century psychologist, was widely praised in the field of psychology for his theory of *operant conditioning*. Skinner theorized that all behavior is environmentally influenced by three things: (1) stimulus (the event or action), (2) response (how the influenced person responds to the event or action), and (3) reinforcement (a reward or consequence; Cherry, 2023). He felt that through a process of behavioral reinforcement using punishments and rewards, you can condition anyone to behave the way you intend. Most of Skinner's research was conducted on animals, and most modern psychologists assert that Skinner's model and findings are simplistic, flawed, and in some cases dangerous. Bioethicist George Dvorsky (2014) has declared that Skinner's model dismisses the important reality of human free will—the fact that human beings and animals are different. Dvorsky (2014) also highlights the naive assumption of good intentions on behalf of the influencer and the dangerous theory that human beings should be controlled. There is room to debate the benefits or flaws of Skinner's theories, but what cannot be denied is that the application of his theories in schools has not improved student academic or behavioral performance. In fact, besides a brief period in the 1980s, the academic achievement gaps between student groups within American schools have consistently widened since 1950 (Hess, 2011).

The PLC at Work process is based on a research-backed conclusion that intense and targeted student support, not rewards or consequences, is the best way to respond when students struggle to meet expectations. This system of support has gone by many names, including *pyramid of interventions, multitiered system of support* (*MTSS*), *response to intervention* (*RTI*), and *academic intervention system* (*AIS*). It is imperative that schools create and apply a system of support, whatever they choose to call it. In an article on the importance of RTI in schools, RTI experts Austin Buffum, Mike Mattos, and Chris Weber (2010) note:

> RTI's underlying premise is that schools should not wait until students fall far enough behind to qualify for special education to provide them with the help they need. Instead, schools should provide targeted and systematic intervention to all students as soon as they demonstrate the need.

A school or team moving forward with the development of a comprehensive student support and intervention system might want to become familiar with some essential vocabulary as defined by the Glossary of Education Reform (www.edglossary.org).

- **Academic support:** "A wide variety of instructional methods, educational services, or school resources provided to students in the effort to help them accelerate their learning progress, catch up with their peers, meet learning standards, or generally succeed in school" (Academic support, 2013)

- **Extended learning time:** "Any educational program or strategy intended to increase the amount of time students are learning, especially for the purposes of improving academic achievement and test scores, or reducing learning loss, learning gaps, and achievement gaps" (Expanded learning time, 2013)

- **Learning gap:** "The difference between what a student has learned—i.e., the academic progress [they have] made—and what the student was expected to learn at a certain point in [their] education, such as a particular age or grade level" (Learning gap, 2013)

- **Achievement gap:** "Any significant and persistent disparity in academic performance or educational attainment between different groups of students, such as white students and minorities, for example, or students from higher-income and lower-income households" (Achievement gap, 2013)

Given the data on unfinished learning due to COVID-19 and the historical stubbornness of the academic achievement gaps between student groups in American schools, it seems logical that an effective school would plan to provide targeted assistance for students who require extra support in meeting both academic and behavioral expectations. Unfortunately, we do not always submit to logic. A 2023 survey of one thousand American teachers found that two-thirds of them feel their schools are not doing enough to support struggling students (Heubeck, 2023).

Buffum, Mattos, and Weber (2012) explain that if schools are truly interested in providing effective support for students and ensuring that all students learn at high levels, they will make four commitments. They call these commitments the *four Cs of RTI:*

1. **Collective responsibility:** A shared belief that the primary responsibility of each member of the organization is to ensure high levels of learning for every child. Thinking is guided by the question, Why are we here?

2. **Concentrated instruction:** A systematic process of identifying essential knowledge and skills that all students must master to learn at high levels, and determining specific learning needs for each child to get there. Thinking is guided by the question, Where do we need to go?

3. **Convergent assessment:** An ongoing process of collectively analyzing targeted evidence to determine the specific learning needs of each child and the effectiveness of the instruction that the child receives in meeting these needs. Thinking is guided by the question, Where are we now?

4. **Certain access:** A systematic process that guarantees every student will receive the time and support needed to learn at high levels. Thinking is guided by the question, How do we get every child there? (Buffum et al., 2012, pp. 9–10)

When I was a principal learning about the PLC at Work process for the first time, this third question caused a paradigm shift for me. The idea that it was the school's responsibility to organize and execute a system of student support was a game changer. Implementing a comprehensive system that suited our students' needs became my obsession and, ultimately, it was the most important factor in our school's positive impact on student achievement.

Critical Question Four: How will we enrich and extend the learning for students who are proficient?

Of the four critical questions, question number four is the most neglected. The influence of standardized tests has caused the gold standard of learning proficiency, not mastery. Some scholars argue that the fight for student excellence ended with school accountability based on standardized testing. These policies base school quality on the number of students meeting minimum proficiency on standardized exams; schools have no real incentive to push students to learn beyond basic proficiency (Klein, 2010). In fact, many school district lobbyists have tried to influence legislators to lower the threshold for proficiency so that a student could reach proficiency by getting less than 50 percent of the standardized exam content correct (Peterson & Hess, 2008). Many people would not consider demonstrating proficiency on less than 50 percent of an exam to reflect high levels of learning. So we will need to generate the intrinsic motivation to answer PLC at Work critical question four. Helping students process and think deeply about their learning helps them become better, more well-rounded people.

According to Yvette Jackson (2011), senior scholar of the National Urban Alliance for Effective Education, all students have gifts and schools should organize themselves to identify and activate those gifts. A school should not just plan to respond when students don't learn; it should also organize itself to respond when students demonstrate an ability to extend their learning. Meeting the minimum requirements of the guaranteed and viable curriculum should be the floor, not the ceiling. Once students have demonstrated an understanding of the basics, they are able to make meaning for themselves and apply that knowledge in a deep, rigorous, and personally meaningful way. Most mission statements claim that schools want students to be *lifelong learners*; critical question four provides a gateway to that goal.

When a team or a school organizes to plan how to extend student learning of essential curriculum, the following terms, as defined by the Glossary of Education Reform (www.edglossary.org), are helpful to know.

- **Rigor:** "Instruction, schoolwork, learning experiences, and educational expectations that are academically, intellectually, and personally challenging" (Rigor, 2014)

- **Critical thinking:** "A term used by educators to describe forms of learning, thought, and analysis that go beyond the memorization and recall of information and facts" (Critical thinking, 2013)

- **Relevance:** "Learning experiences that are either directly applicable to the personal aspirations, interests, or cultural experiences of students (*personal relevance*) or that are connected in some way to real-world issues, problems, and contexts (*life relevance*)" (Relevance, 2013)

- **Personalized learning:** "A diverse variety of educational programs, learning experiences, instructional approaches, and academic support strategies that are intended to address the distinct learning needs, interests, aspirations, or cultural backgrounds of individual students" (Personalized learning, 2015)

In their book *When They Already Know It: How to Extend and Personalize Student Learning in a PLC at Work*, Mark Weichel, Blane McCann, and Tami Williams (2018) argue that personalized learning is the gateway to truly achieving high levels of learning for all students, and a team's commitment to critical question four is paramount. These authors identify five elements of this commitment that are needed to successfully advance personalized learning.

1. Know your learners.
2. Allow voice and choice.
3. Implement flexibility.
4. Effectively use data.
5. Integrate technology.

This book also provides a wealth of instructional practices to help teams strategically achieve the goals of personalizing and extending student learning. We cannot view high levels of learning by meeting minimum expectations.

BIG IDEA TWO: A COLLABORATIVE CULTURE

Working with like-minded people who have common objectives is an effective and efficient way to ensure a high level of learning for each student. The architects of the

PLC at Work process write, "The second big idea driving the PLC process is that in order to ensure all students learn at high levels, educators must work collaboratively and take collective responsibility for the success of each student" (DuFour et al., 2016, p. 11). What struck me upon first learning about the four critical questions of a PLC at Work is that the pronoun *we* is part of every critical question. I think most educators would agree that identifying what is essential to learn, gathering evidence on student progress, and providing support or extended learning opportunities for students represent good practice. Teachers do these things individually all the time. What makes the PLC at Work process magical is that we agree to do these things *together*.

Teams Versus Groups

There are many ways to collaborate, but the platform advocated by the PLC at Work process is the collaborative team. A team is different from a group or a committee. Merriam-Webster defines a *team* as "a number of persons associated together in work or activity, such as a group on one side" (Team, n.d.). Richard DuFour and Rebecca DuFour (2006) assert that a team is held together by three essential elements: (1) interdependence, (2) common goals, and (3) mutual accountability. Being a team is more than working in proximity to other people. Members of a team are passionate about a common cause, and they agree to a set of behaviors each person will contribute to achieve the team's goal. In the case of education, the goal is securing high levels of learning for all students.

Teaming does more than provide a group of companions who share the same passion; it also increases capacity, individually and collectively. A term generally associated with the increased capacity developed through good collaboration is *collective intelligence*, commonly defined as shared or group intelligence that emerges from the collaboration, collective efforts, and competition of many individuals and appears in consensus decision making (Suran, Pattanaik, & Draheim, 2020). In a study published in 2010, researchers assessed the effectiveness and individual and collective intelligence of 192 groups by giving the groups complex tasks to complete. The researchers found that the groups with the highest collective intelligence scores performed much better than groups with high individual intelligence scores but low collective intelligence scores. Therefore, the researchers concluded that collective intelligence is more powerful than aggregated individual intelligence (Woolley, Chabris, Pentland, Hashmi, & Malone, 2010).

Mental Health and Retention

As explored in the previous chapter, both students' and teachers' mental and emotional health are at a breaking point since the COVID-19 pandemic. Schools have always had their teacher stressors—teaching, planning, managing classrooms, managing time, and managing parents and the community—but the current challenges are unprecedented. Perhaps our system of educator isolation has lost its value both professionally and emotionally.

Singapore, one of the highest-performing nations in the world academically, has chosen a different approach to teacher working conditions and professional expectations (Walker, 2016). In Singapore, a teacher workweek is 47.6 hours on average, and a teacher spends approximately 17.1 hours engaged in classroom instruction. This reduced student instructional time for teachers is made possible through a national investment in increasing teacher staffing in each school. Singaporean schools have a lower teacher-to-student ratio than U.S. schools, which allows Singaporean teachers to spend more time developing their professional craft. The hours not spent in classrooms are generally spent working in collaborative teams, observing other teachers, and designing lessons. In the United States, a teacher workweek is 44.8 hours on average, and a teacher spends approximately 26.8 hours engaged in classroom instruction. Only Chilean teachers allocate more instructional time than American teachers do. Singaporean education officials credit their collaborative culture with high job satisfaction rates and low attrition rates among their teachers.

There are American schools enjoying some of the same benefits of a collaborative culture. For example, Colleyville Middle School in Colleyville, Texas, has been able to retain its staff, and also has received a Schools to Watch designation by the Association for Middle Level Education (AMLE; Superville, 2023). Many teachers at this school commute more than an hour to work each day, and many have turned down pay raise opportunities at other schools to stay. The educators stay at this school because of the collaborative culture, the focus on professional growth, and the commitment to celebrating both teachers and students. These characteristics can be duplicated by any school or district that chooses to value these principles. A 2022 study found that if schools want to recover from the impact of the COVID-19 pandemic and thrive in the future, they need to create a culture of collaboration and shared decision making (McCarthy, Blaydes, Weppner, & Lambert, 2022).

In addition to benefiting schools by improving professional practice, collaboration is an important component in recruiting, developing, and retaining quality teachers.

We face a crisis on many fronts in this modern era. Working together, instead of working alone, is an efficient and effective way forward. Wouldn't it make sense for schools and school districts to reshape their school structures so teachers have time to meaningfully collaborate? Wouldn't it also make sense to primarily spend that time on answering the four critical questions of a PLC at Work? Some things are timeless. Working together will never go out of style and should be a staple in any high-performing organization, especially a school.

BIG IDEA THREE: A RESULTS ORIENTATION

Because the primary purpose of schooling is to ensure student learning, schools and school systems must monitor the indicators of learning. It is difficult to understand the success of an organization if the bottom line is rarely collected, analyzed, and acted on. A business that never monitors its sales data, market share, and customer satisfaction will probably be out of business relatively soon. What has been obvious in other professions has not always been so obvious in the field of education.

Harvard University professor emeritus of education Richard Elmore (2000), in a critique of American school improvement, accused leaders of creating a buffer between its educators and the reality of their impact:

> Administration in education . . . has come to mean not the management of instruction but the management of the structures and processes around instruction. That which cannot be directly managed must, in this view, be protected from external scrutiny. Buffering consists of creating structures and procedures around the technical core of teaching that, at the same time, (1) protect teachers from outside intrusions in their highly uncertain and murky work, and (2) create the appearance of rational management of the technical core, so as to allay the uncertainties of the public about the actual quality or legitimacy of what is happening in the technical core. (p. 6)

In the previous chapter, I shared evidence that educators are more emotionally fragile and traumatized today than at any other time in our public school journey. COVID-19's impact on both students and educators, coupled with external political, social, and economic forces, might lead us to create even more buffers to discomfort. We must remove these buffers, and though it will be uncomfortable, it doesn't have to be excruciating if we do it correctly. In his book *The Five Dysfunctions of a Team: A Leadership Fable*, Patrick Lencioni (2002) warns there are five behaviors that can undermine the potency of a team. One of those destructive habits is *fear of conflict*, which leads to what he describes as *artificial harmony*. This behavior robs a team of reflecting on the impact of their behavior and freezes their ability to improve. What makes this behavior shortsighted is the fact that human beings are ultimately driven by an intrinsic need to make a positive difference (Pink, 2011). Discomfort and improvement are eternally connected.

The PLC at Work process recognizes the need for the system to have a results orientation to effectively improve student learning. "The third big idea that drives the work of PLCs is the need for a results orientation. To assess their effectiveness in helping all students learn, educators in a PLC focus on results—evidence of student learning" (DuFour et al., 2016, p. 12). Monitoring objective evidence of each student's progress is essential to producing an environment where all students learn at high levels. Any evidence that helps us improve our impact on student learning is welcome in a PLC at Work.

In my more than thirty years of teaching in and leading schools, I always wondered why my colleagues were so sensitive to unfavorable feedback. If we are truly trying to improve our impact on students, we need to look for areas of improvement. Jim Collins (2001), in his book *Good to Great: Why Some Companies Make the Leap . . . and Others Don't*, explores why iconic companies in history have been able to reach unprecedented heights of success. One characteristic of these companies is their ability to seek and confront what he calls *brutal facts*. These represent evidence that is unfavorable and uncomfortable but revealing. This information lights the pathway for improvement if properly analyzed. Collins (2001) writes:

> When you start with an honest and diligent effort to determine the truth of your situation, the right decisions often become self-evident. It is impossible to make good decisions without infusing the entire process with an honest confrontation of the brutal facts. (p. 88)

The emotional state of educators, especially in the current context, is a real concern. But the record learning gaps that students face are equally real and of concern. How do we create a results orientation to monitor and close the learning gaps of students, yet still honor the emotional needs of educators? As Lencioni (2002) points out, avoiding conflict and engaging in artificial harmony do not help. In their book *Leading Schools in a Data-Rich World*, Lorna Earl and Steven Katz (2006) say that since the inception of test-based school accountability, educators have carried a general fear of data, which they call *data anxiety*. Earl and Katz (2006) argue that the concept of accountability needs to be redefined in order for this anxiety or fear of data to change. If we use data formatively to improve student performance, it makes sense to use data formatively to improve educator performance:

> High-stakes accountability systems can create a sense of urgency and provide "pressure" for change. However, real accountability is much more than accounting. . . . It is a moral and professional responsibility to be knowledgeable and fair in teaching and in interactions with students and their parents. It engenders respect, trust, shared understanding, and mutual support. (Earl & Katz, 2006, p. 10)

Focusing on the critical needs of students, when done properly, should not be debilitating for educators or stimulate shame or disrespect. Research has proven that if we redefine accountability as being knowledgeable of students' needs and acting accordingly, it should create passion instead of anxiety (Holcomb, 2012). We cannot afford to exchange professional improvement for artificial harmony.

Conclusion

As we find ourselves in the wilderness of the aftermath of COVID-19, we face monumental challenges. We have to confront mental health issues for both educators and students, record losses in student achievement, an educator shortage, and disruptive social and political forces. Perhaps PLC at Work, the concept first introduced in 1998, can be the way forward out of these dilemmas and provide a path to future prosperity. Richard DuFour and Robert Eaker did not create the concept of professional learning communities, but they did create a logical framework that would define the work that educators do in a PLC. This work can be summarized in three big ideas: (1) a focus on learning, (2) a collaborative culture, and (3) a results orientation.

The fundamental purpose of a school is to improve learning for students. To do that, the educators in the school need to have a collaborative focus on learning. In the PLC at Work process, they achieve that by answering four critical questions: (1) What do we want students to learn? (2) How will we know if they are learning? (3) How will we respond when students don't learn? and (4) How will we respond when students have learned? Some benefits of answering these questions include the following.

- Teachers involved in creating a guaranteed and viable curriculum will be more effective at improving their individual and collective practice. They will also enjoy greater job satisfaction and be personally invested in the standards and learning outcomes that they choose, compared to teachers whose standards and learning outcomes are exclusively chosen by others.

- Teachers involved in creating and implementing common formative assessments will be more effective at improving student learning. They will get an opportunity to reflect on the effectiveness of their own professional practice, learn strategies from colleagues, test professional theories, and share their expertise with others.

- Teachers involved in the development and implementation of a system of student support and extension are more likely to improve student learning. Collectively providing student support reduces personal and professional stress and anxiety for teachers and has proven to be more effective than having individual teachers provide students with support or extended opportunities.

Schools work better when educators work together toward a common goal.

A collaborative culture is essential in improving student learning. Schools have historically had teachers work in isolation, but a wealth of research has taught us that working together is more effective and efficient. Some benefits include the following.

- Teachers who work on strong collaborative teams have higher job satisfaction. Instead of engaging in "hunting exhibitions" to vent dissatisfaction, they work as a team to support one another to find solutions.

- Teachers who work in a collaborative culture grow professionally and feel compelled to stay longer than those who work in isolation.

- Improving individual and collective intelligence creates a culture of continuous improvement.

- A collaborative culture helps accelerate the learning curve for new teachers and may be beneficial for new teachers who have not taken the traditional route of teacher education to enter the field. This reality is most evident in urban and rural school districts.

A school committed to the PLC at Work process has a results orientation. The teams of teachers do not run from their challenges; they tackle them together. Confronting brutal facts is a critical characteristic of a high-performing organization, and PLC at Work schools do not seek to create a buffer between themselves and their current realities. Rather, they collaborate with a moral purpose to solve those realities. *Accountability* is not a synonym for *punishment*—it is a passionate call for action. Some benefits of a results orientation include:

- Avoiding artificial harmony and producing a sense of intrinsic satisfaction, which is the ultimate motivator of human behavior

- Developing a culture of vision stimulated by evidence, which targets and strengthens improvement efforts

- Encouraging risk-taking, experimentation, and innovation without the fear of punishment and shame, which builds ownership

If we would have collectively committed to these principles in 1998, maybe COVID-19's impact on our profession would not have been so severe. But the good news is that it is not too late! We can still act with a sense of urgency because our profession and community depend on it. In the next chapter, we will move from a theoretical understanding of PLC at Work to a real plan of action to make it the norm in every school and every school district.

Pause to Think and Plan

Amen!

Aha!

So What?

CHAPTER 5

Staying the Course— Are We Engaged In PLC Right or PLC Lite?

In the previous chapter, I sought to prove that the PLC at Work process is the culmination of an evolving knowledge base on how to collaboratively improve schools through an intense focus on student learning. That process has tangibly improved schools and positively affected students all over the world. The beauty of the process is that it is accessible to any school that desires to fully engage. As I expressed in the introduction, partial or pseudo engagement in the process was unfinished business for Rick DuFour when he left us in 2017. I am counting on the readers of this book to join me in finishing the journey.

If schools were truly committed to fully implementing the PLC at Work process with a razor-sharp focus on student learning, they would commit to the following:

1. Educators work collaboratively rather than in isolation, take collective responsibility for student learning,

and clarify the commitments they make to each other about how they will work together.

2.   The fundamental structure of the school becomes the collaborative team in which members work interdependently to achieve common goals for which all members are mutually accountable.

3.   The team establishes a guaranteed and viable curriculum, unit by unit, so all students have access to the same knowledge and skills regardless of the teacher to whom they are assigned.

4.   The team develops common formative assessments to frequently gather evidence of student learning.

5.   The school has created a system of interventions and extensions to ensure students who struggle receive additional time and support for learning in a way that is timely, directive, diagnostic, and systematic, and students who demonstrate proficiency can extend their learning.

6.   The team uses evidence of student learning to inform and improve the individual and collective practice of its members. (DuFour et al., 2016, p. 14)

DuFour and Eaker often refer to these elements as the "tight elements" of the PLC at Work process. For the purpose of this book, I'd like to refer to these commitments as *PLC Right*. When schools are fully engaged in this process, these behaviors are the right work. The body of research that I cited in the previous chapter supports the notion that educators deeply involved in this work increase the likelihood of drastically improving student learning and create a more satisfying environment for the professionals within their schools.

Unfortunately, many stop short of achieving PLC Right. There are many challenges on the road to drastically changing our professional practice, and in most cases, educators will settle for *PLC Lite*:

Although many schools around the world have claimed to embrace the professional learning community (PLC) process, it

> would be more accurate to describe the current state of affairs in many schools as PLC Lite. . . . [PLC Lite fails] to embrace the central tenets of the PLC process and won't lead to higher levels of learning for students or adults. (DuFour & Reeves, 2016, p. 69)

PLC Right requires a monumental shift in practice, and the challenges are uncomfortable and ongoing, but anything that is valuable is difficult in some way. Are we willing to embrace the difficulty to save our profession and lay the groundwork for future prosperity?

> Reculturing schools and school districts into high-performing PLCs is a difficult and complex journey. While there is no one way to proceed on the journey, there are certain steps—stops along the way—that schools must address. Educators must work to create and truly embrace a clear and compelling purpose—a focus on high levels of learning for all students. (Mattos, DuFour, DuFour, Eaker, & Many, 2016, p. 151)

If your own child, or a child you love, were suffering and you were given access to a remedy that would heal them, would you take that journey no matter how difficult? I believe all of us would make that journey. The goal of this book is not to convince you to fall in love with PLC. The goal is to rekindle your fire for student learning and to make the case that the PLC at Work process is our best means to ensure that all students learn. If you can articulate a more logical, practical, and research-affirmed way to achieve that, you have my attention. If not, let's go on the PLC journey and persevere until we reach our destination.

The Journey

Those of us who champion the PLC at Work process often describe a school's attempts to implement the process as their *PLC journey*. Rick DuFour (2015) wrote:

> The journey will undoubtedly require hard work. But if there is one undeniable reality for every educator every year, it is that we are going to work hard. . . . Will we work hard and succeed or work hard and fail? Working tirelessly and failing creates despair and drives good, talented people out of our profession.

> But working hard and seeing the fruits of our efforts—seeing
> more students learn and succeed—are what draw people to this
> profession. (p. 252)

There has never been a better time to make up our minds to make this journey. We have been exposed to this process for twenty-five years. It is time to stop making excuses and actually *do* what the evidence has shown is best.

We often get angry when noneducators criticize our profession. We feel attacked and disrespected. But it is difficult for that anger to be justifiable if we don't self-analyze and self-correct. In his book *Results Now: How We Can Achieve Unprecedented Improvements in Teaching and Learning*, Mike Schmoker (2006) writes that "educators in overwhelming majorities have agreed that there is indeed a yawning gap between the most well-known, incontestably essential practices and the reality of most class-rooms" (p. 2). No one has forbidden us from engaging in the critical commitments and practices of PLC Right; we have by and large chosen to ignore the reality of our disconnect. "Excellent schools deliver a clear message to their students: No Excuses" (Thernstrom & Thernstrom, 2003, p. 272). Can we truly send this message to students and ignore it ourselves?

COMMITMENT ISSUES

Commitment to a process is paramount if we want to benefit from the process. One of the greatest mysteries in life is that most human beings are fully aware of the pathways to success but rarely fully engage in them. A person promotes good health when they eat healthy foods and exercise; a person becomes more financially secure when they spend less money than they earn. This dilemma is often called the *knowing-doing gap* (Pfeffer & Sutton, 2000). This is prevalent in PLC implementation too. In their book *Starting a Movement: Building Culture From the Inside Out in Professional Learning Communities*, Ken Williams and Tom Hierck (2015) note:

> We have seen many schools in which the staff believe they're
> implementing the PLC process effectively. In reality, we
> instead find patterns, habits, and actions that fall short of
> the commitment required for PLCs to be embedded into the
> culture. (p. 96)

Instead of fully committing, many schools make partial commitments or are engaged in various stages of PLC Lite (Williams & Hierck, 2015).

1. **Flirting with PLC:** These schools are engaged in surface-level implementation bred out of a demand to comply instead of intrinsic motivation. Passion is absent on most teams, and excuses are prevalent.

2. **Dating PLC:** These schools are more engaged and not simply "flirting" with PLC. Teams can produce some artifacts of the process and even some preliminary evidence of student growth. But there is still some unresolved doubt that prevents full, universal commitment.

3. **Engaged to PLC:** These schools have "put a ring on it" and made a public declaration of their intent to fully commit. They are honest and sincere in their efforts, and they are striving to make a perfect union. They are on the PLC path and intend to stay on the path.

Have you made up your mind to put a ring on your commitment to PLC and give the process a sincere effort? We can move beyond our commitment issues. No excuses!

SMALL SCHOOLS AND SINGLETONS

If you teach in a small school or are a singleton, you might be thinking, *How can we collaborate? We are such a small school, and no one else teaches what I teach.* I established in the previous chapter that a wealth of research concludes teachers improve their practice when they work with others. There's no denying that being in proximity to someone who teaches the same thing that you teach would be a convenient reality for collaborating. But there are schools and districts all over the world that have committed to the PLC at Work process and have created strong collaborative cultures despite their small staffs.

Time is a precious asset for teachers; many would argue it is their most precious asset. The job of educating students is rigorous, and teachers have a low tolerance for poorly used time. Aaron Hansen, an award-winning former principal from the state of Nevada, successfully led the PLC process at a small rural school. In *How to Develop PLCs for Singletons and Small Schools* (Hansen, 2015), he writes:

> If you have felt marginalized in some way, I want to challenge you [singleton teachers] to assume good intentions. It is highly unlikely that your principal, and those working with [them] to help establish the PLC framework, thought, "Let's see how we

can make some people feel devalued." Instead, assume that they just didn't know how to include you—yet. (p. 3)

Hansen (2015) suggests some alternative team structures that have the potential to fully engage the singleton teacher in a robust, collaborative professional life.

- Vertical teams

- Interdisciplinary teams

- Singletons who support

- Virtual teams

- Structural change

Though these suggestions may not be as convenient as sharing with someone who has the exact same job responsibilities as you, they can be equally beneficial. The AllThingsPLC website (www.allthingsplc.info) features scores of schools that have created a collaborative culture in a small school environment. Reach out to some of them and get some advice if this is your most prevalent excuse for PLC Lite.

Brig Leane and Jon Yost (2022) provide some additional guidance in this area in their book *Singletons in a PLC at Work*. They suggest that every staff member can find their way onto a strong collaborative team by choosing the most beneficial "on-ramp":

> The term *on-ramp* refers to how to get started in meaningful collaboration. Specifically, singleton teachers use the term *on-ramp* to answer the following questions:
>
> 1. With whom should I collaborate?
>
> 2. What specific tasks should my team engage in?
>
> 3. What templates or protocols should my team utilize to guide our work? (Leane & Yost, 2022, p. 17)

Leane and Yost go on to describe three possible on-ramps that singleton teachers might use to find a pathway to meaningful collaboration.

1. **Course-alike on-ramp:** People who teach what you teach but work in different locations

2. **Common-content on-ramp:** People who teach the same subject but at different levels, like a vertical team

3. **Critical-friend on-ramp:** People who teach a different subject but might face a common problem of practice

They conclude that anyone who truly wants to benefit from the process of collaboration can do it. No excuses!

SPECIAL EDUCATION

Having high learning expectations for all students includes having high expectations for students enrolled in special education. In chapter 2 (page 23), we reviewed the journey of students with disabilities in the United States. It has been a rocky journey, to say the least. But years of lobbying and the work of activists have led to laws, regulations, and funding aimed at including these students and improving their learning outcomes. Unfortunately, the work is far from over. In an *Education Week* article titled "Special Education Is Broken," Christina A. Samuels (2019) writes, "Children with disabilities aren't always identified for needs when they have them. When they are identified, what happens in the classroom is hit-or-miss." Students identified for special education services have traditionally been segregated from their general education peers, and special education teachers have tried to meet their students' needs in isolation, as opposed to collaborating with their general education teacher peers. This tradition has created conditions that are more likely to slow student academic growth than to accelerate it (Ballis & Heath, 2021). Could the PLC at Work process be a pathway to a better future for special education students?

While serving as leaders in Kildeer Countryside Community Consolidated School District 96 in Buffalo Grove, Illinois, Heather Friziellie, Julie Schmidt, and Jeanne Spiller facilitated thirteen years of continuous achievement growth for students with disabilities. Their school district has been a model PLC and lighthouse for others seeking to secure continuous growth. How were these three leaders so successful? In their book *Yes We Can! General and Special Educators Collaborating in a Professional Learning Community*, they assert that the traditional system is a "'wait to fail' instead of a model based on prevention and intervention" (Friziellie, Schmidt, & Spiller, 2016, p. 10). They used the PLC process to make three critical commitments that led to their success.

1. Focus more on results and focus less on process.

2. Embrace a model of prevention and not a model of failure.

3. Think of students with special needs as general education students first and special education students second in classrooms and in boardrooms.

In *Yes We Can!*, Friziellie, Schmidt, and Spiller (2016) provide stellar insight and advice, along with easily duplicable tools and strategies that special education teams and officials can utilize to truly commit to learning equity for special education students. What we have traditionally done has clearly not worked; why not try a different approach? No excuses!

URBAN SCHOOLS AND THE CHALLENGES OF POVERTY

Another convenient justification to not fully engage in the PLC at Work process is the belief that issues related to race, poverty, and culture excuse us from expecting high academic performance from all students. I spent nineteen years as an urban educator, and the challenges that poverty, racial discrimination, and generational self-hate can bring are real. The research is clear that school success is easier when students come from financially stable homes led by educated parents who regularly communicate in academic language (Winerip, 2007). In his book *Poor Students, Rich Teaching: Mindsets for Change*, Eric Jensen (2016) defines poverty as "a chronic experience resulting from an aggregate of adverse social and economic risk factors" (p. 6). Jensen (2016) offers some guidance on how schools should proceed to address the barrier of poverty in a student's learning journey:

> Ignore the political, social, and economic "noise" out there, and focus on helping each of your students graduate. Nothing moves forward when we complain about what we don't have, how we are undervalued, and how we work with some who poison our school culture. Things only move forward when you focus on the path of success for your students. (p. 1)

The victim mentality does not equip a professional with the mindset or focus necessary to confront their challenges. Poverty is challenging and disruptive to the learning process, but it is no match for a focused, optimistic group of educators.

Bo Ryan is the principal of Ana Grace Academy of the Arts Middle School, a magnet school in Bloomfield, Connecticut. Bloomfield is in the metro Hartford area, which is one of the most economically depressed areas in New England, and notorious for violence (Wilson & Stamp, 2022). Thousands of schools across the United States and the world face similar dilemmas. As Jensen (2016) advises these schools to do, Ryan and the staff at Ana Grace Academy decided to take action instead of complain about their circumstances. And this school has been honored as a Model PLC school, which means it has made continuous growth in critical areas of student learning for at least three years. Ryan and his staff use the PLC at Work process as their vehicle for improving student learning.

How have they done it? In his book *The Brilliance in the Building: Effecting Change in Urban Schools With the PLC at Work Process*, Ryan (2023) details their approach to mitigating the impact of poverty and despair, outlining five critical steps.

1. **Shift to a culture of care:** Change starts with us.

2. **Create a culture of collaboration:** We can't do this alone.

3. **Focus on learning:** Make the main thing the main thing.

4. **Provide high-quality instruction:** Our kids don't stand a chance without it.

5. **Promote continuous learning:** We can't do better if we don't know better.

Like the other books I have referenced, this book is full of sage advice, practical strategies, and templates that schools facing some of the same challenges as Ana Grace Academy can use. The PLC at Work process improves outcomes for students of all income levels, races, and home languages. We can reach these students. No excuses!

Solution Tree has provided a free, valuable resource to assist any school seeking to fully commit to the PLC process: the AllThingsPLC website (www.allthingsplc.info). There, you can find a comprehensive list of schools and districts that have resolved some of the most prevalent excuses to settling for PLC Lite. Feel free to review the model schools and find some just like yours. Reach out to them, ask them questions, and even schedule visits. They likely can provide you with suggestions and possible solutions to your challenges. In this modern era, there is no real excuse for PLC Lite.

The Challenge of Change

I have found that most schools stop short of their PLC destination not because they misunderstand the concepts or don't have access to the right tools but because they do not understand organizational change, or they are not invested enough in the goal of improving student learning to endure the discomfort of the journey. This reality is what moved me to spend most of my time as an author and consultant on the topic of transforming school culture.

School change is multidimensional. It happens at two levels. I call these two dimensions of change *technical change* and *cultural change* (Muhammad, 2018). "Technical changes are changes to the tools or mechanisms professionals use to do their jobs effectively" (Muhammad, 2018, p. 22). Technical changes are important. Effective improvement requires consistent analysis and action in relation to curriculum, time for tasks (like collaboration), protocols, policies, and technology. Technical change will always be necessary because systemic challenges will always change and evolve, and the tools needed to respond will have to change as well. In addition, creating technical change can be time consuming. When I was a principal in the early 2000s, before the mass adoption of smartphones, I could not have imagined how cell phones and social media would consume people's time and attention and demand policy development in modern schools. A school would be wise to consider the number of proposed technical changes assigned to educators as it plans its improvement journey. Robert Marzano and Timothy Waters (2009) find that when school systems try to institute too many technical changes simultaneously, the sheer scope can overwhelm practitioners and create an aversion to change itself. According to leadership experts Terrence E. Deal and Kent D. Peterson (2016), cultural change involves actively influencing a school's "complex webs of stories, traditions, and rituals" (p. 8). Effective systemic transformation requires a strategic focus on both dimensions of change: technical and cultural. Of the two forms of organizational change, changing culture is the more challenging. Any leader considering the full adoption of the PLC at Work process should gain a comprehensive understanding of cultural change.

I often hear educators use the words *culture* and *climate* interchangeably. These two concepts are profoundly different. In summary, climate is how we *feel* and culture is how we *behave*. Education experts Steve Gruenert and Todd Whitaker (2015) write that "culture is 'the way we do things around here' and climate is 'the way we feel around here'" (p. 10). A group of educators might feel good about themselves and their school community but still behave in ways that are unproductive.

For visualization purposes, I would like you to consider both forms of change in the following context. If a person desires to cultivate a productive garden, two key elements will be apparent: (1) prepared soil and (2) suitable seeds? The gardener will need to prepare the garden's soil to have high confidence that the planted seeds will germinate and blossom. So when considering organizational change, think of technical change as gathering the right *seeds* and cultural change as preparing the right *soil* conditions. Both are essential to achieve a bountiful harvest, but one task is much more difficult than the other. It takes a lot of sweat equity, strenuous labor, and patience to till, fertilize, and hydrate soil. If a gardener is not willing to commit to this work and places seeds in bad soil, they are highly unlikely to reap a good harvest. I often witness schools thinking that they can cheat the change process and compensate for their unwillingness to cultivate their culture by seeking a technical change that might be a shortcut.

Change does not allow for shortcuts! We must engage in both dimensions. Deal and Peterson (1999) write that:

> Educators are being pressured by policy makers to adopt practices that many of the best organizations shy away from. If schools want to emulate other successful organizations, then parents, teachers, and administrators need to take a look at their local traditions, folkways, and dreams. And this look has to be sustained, fine-grained scrutiny, not a brief superficial glance. (p. 4)

This sustained effort to improve culture results in what I call a *positive school culture*. A positive culture is a place where:

- Educators have an unwavering belief in the ability of all of their students to achieve success, and they pass that belief on to others in overt and covert ways.

- Educators create policies and procedures and adopt practices that support their belief in the ability of every student. (Muhammad, 2009, p. 13)

Creating this type of environment would greatly enhance the improvement process. Impatience with cultural change and haste to mandate technical changes have doomed many schools in their improvement journeys.

Patrick Lencioni (2012), in his book *The Advantage: Why Organizational Health Trumps Everything Else in Business*, examines why some companies make great strides in the marketplace but others don't. His findings mirror mine; we just use different vocabulary. He finds that companies have two dimensions of change, which he calls the *health* (cultural) and *smart* (technical) dimensions. According to Lencioni (2012), the companies that focus on building their health (culture) to provide a context for implementing their smart (technical) innovations are much more successful than those that ignore their health. He warns that leadership's aversion to the inconvenience of change resistance will be an organization's greatest obstacle to improvement. He notes:

> Most leaders prefer to look for answers where the light is better, where they are more comfortable. And the light is certainly better in the measurable, objective, and data-driven world of organizational intelligence (the smart side of the equation) than it is in the messier, more unpredictable world of organizational health. (Lencioni, 2012, p. 7)

Courageous, moral leadership presents our best chance to change culture. As I have coached and guided schools since 2002, I have seen the impact of leaders who refuse to address culture—PLC Lite.

PLC Reboots

Because the PLC at Work movement has been in motion for twenty-five years, it is rare that an educator has never heard of the concept. There are hundreds of books, along with live and virtual opportunities, to learn about the process. Richard DuFour and Robert Eaker had to build a team of PLC associates to keep up with the demand in the field to learn about this process. Just before the COVID-19 pandemic, my colleagues and I started to get requests to go to schools or school districts that were asking for a "PLC reboot." These requests have continued to grow since COVID-19 restrictions were lifted.

What is a *PLC reboot*? It occurs in a school or school district that previously invested money or time in the PLC at Work process but did not have the courage to align its culture and systems with the process's demands and, as a result, educators wasted collaborative time or developed a negative impression of the process. The reboot happens when this school wants to hire a speaker to get people excited again. But before you can successfully launch a reboot, a thorough examination of why the last "boot" didn't work is in order. It is likely the last implementation of the PLC process failed because of a misunderstanding or lack of knowledge among leadership about the cultural conditions necessary to successfully implement and sustain PLC.

Time for Change Framework

In 2019, I coauthored a book with Luis Cruz titled *Time for Change: Four Essential Skills for Transformational School and District Leaders* (Muhammad & Cruz, 2019). Our goal with the book was to help leaders solve a quandary posed by Richard DuFour and Michael Fullan (2013):

> How should leaders engage people in the complex process of cultural change? Should they be *tight*—assertive, issuing top-down directives that mandate change? Or should they be *loose*—merely encouraging people to engage in the change process, but leaving participation optional? The challenge at all levels of the system is to navigate this apparent dichotomy and find the appropriate balance between tight and loose, between assertiveness and autonomy. If we know anything about change, it is that ordering people to change doesn't work, nor does leaving them alone. (p. 33)

Effective leadership can greatly accelerate the pace of effective cultural change. It used to be generally assumed that real systemic change takes three to five years. However, Douglas Reeves and Robert Eaker (2019) find that achieving real, tangible change can take as little as one hundred days. Maybe cultural change took so long because we didn't know enough about it, or we just chose to use the wrong tools. As our current reality in the field of education indicates (see chapter 3, page 43), we don't have three to five years to wait on the slow pace of change we've traditionally tolerated.

This is why Cruz and I wrote *Time for Change*. We wrote, "Our goal with this book is to provide leaders with a logical and duplicable process so that anyone who wants to become an effective school leader has a road map for success" (Muhammad & Cruz, 2019, p. 2). Instead of using the terms *loose* and *tight* as DuFour and Fullan (2013) do to define the necessary leadership balance for change, we use the terms *support* and *accountability*. We further distinguish these two realities by describing them as *investments* (support) and a *return* (accountability). The golden rule of leading cultural change is that you cannot expect a return from your culture if you have not first made the proper investments. In turn, it is perfectly logical to expect a return on your investments if you have made the proper investments. If leaders can maintain this delicate balance, they greatly increase the likelihood of producing a healthy school culture.

Cruz and I argue that leaders must simultaneously exhibit four critical skills in order to accelerate cultural change. Those behaviors are (1) *communicating*, (2) *building trust*, (3) *building capacity*, and (4) *having accountability*. We suggest that leaders take the following approach when pursuing cultural change:

1. **Leaders must effectively communicate the rationale—the *why* of the work:** People tend to resist change to practice and lack motivation to improve when leaders have not skillfully communicated their rationale or case for improvement. To embrace a vision, people have to clearly understand the vision and feel personally compelled to contribute to the vision.

2. **Leaders must effectively establish trust—the *who* of the work:** A transformational leader needs the essential ability to connect with others' emotions. Facts and objective evidence alone do not inspire people; people need to connect with their leader on a personal level and know that their leader has not just made an intellectual connection but also an ethical connection to their purpose.

3. **Leaders must effectively build capacity—the *how* of the work:** People will more willingly take a risk and try a new idea if leaders have prepared them professionally. Leaders must invest in training, resources, and time if they want educators to enthusiastically embrace new ideas and practices.

4. **Leaders must get results—the *do* of the work:** Ultimately, improvement cannot be optional. A transformational leader must skillfully assess and meet the needs of those that [they lead], but eventually, [they have] to demand full participation in the change and improvement process. (Muhammad & Cruz, 2019, p. 6)

Leadership is critical to any attempt to nurture change, and it is critical for *PLC Right*. Think of leadership not as a position but rather as a set of responsibilities to be shared collaboratively. We have known for years that collaborative leadership is more effective than autocratic leadership (Katzenmeyer & Moller, 2009). Included in the appendix of this book (page 145) is a tool that will help you monitor these critical leadership behaviors as you move forward in this process. You might find that resistance is a result of inattention to one of the critical components of change leadership. I suggest that you use this tool as a guide to make sure that your implementation is simultaneously loose and tight.

I am not suggesting that the PLC process needs a hero leader who naturally embodies all the transformational characteristics of effective leadership in order to create the proper culture. I am suggesting that a group of ordinary people can be influential if they pool their collective intelligence and work together to lead this process. Schools engaged in the PLC journey commonly refer to this group of leaders as a *guiding coalition.*

When I approached Richard DuFour in 2001 as a bright-eyed young principal, I was eager to go back to my school and just go to work. He cautioned me against being overzealous and advised me to build a coalition of advocates and approach the shift as a collective instead as the lone advocate of this new process. He advised that I put together a team that would lead the school through this massive transition from professional isolation to professional collaboration. He referred to the team as a guiding coalition. The term was unfamiliar to me at the time, but I followed his advice and created a team that would prove to be invaluable in our improvement efforts.

Schools have always had teams assigned for school improvement. Often, these teams are called *leadership teams, school-improvement teams,* or *site committees.* The name of the team is not really important; how that team functions is what is most important. The term *guiding coalition* is credited to leadership and change expert John Kotter (2012). He asserts that organizations that succeed at cultivating real change do so collaboratively. He advises choosing members of this important team based on the following qualifications.

- **Positional power:** Someone with a title or positional authority
- **Expertise:** Someone with a unique skill set that will enhance the team
- **Credibility:** Someone who is respected by peers
- **Leadership ability:** Someone who takes initiative without a title

These guidelines will help schools choose a balanced group of team members who truly represent the diversity of the staff.

In *Powerful Guiding Coalitions: How to Build and Sustain the Leadership Team in Your PLC at Work,* Bill Hall (2022) defines a guiding coalition as "an alliance of staff from within a school who have the responsibility of leading a change process through the many challenges and barriers of implementation" (p. 9). As a principal who led this process, I can verify that Hall's definition is accurate. There were challenges and barriers to my school's PLC journey, and you will experience your own challenges. Hall (2022) notes that the guiding coalition focuses on learning for both students and professionals. Issues like student behavior, tardy policies, and school dismissal procedures are best handled by a different team in a different way. Deviating from the theme of learning can cause the guiding coalition to drift from its fundamental purpose.

Having a strong guiding coalition was essential to our success at Levey Middle School. No critical learning decision was made without our first vetting it through this team. Our guiding coalition committed to three principles, which make the acronym *MOM*.

1. **Model:** If we were going to ask the staff to collaborate, we had an obligation to model good collaboration.

2. **Organize:** The logistics of creating systems, structures, templates, and processes are laborious. The dirty work occupied most of our time.

3. **Monitor:** For us to give the staff proper support, monitoring implementation and impact was essential. We were in charge of the loose-tight balance.

As you move into implementation, use the guiding coalition to support and monitor each phase. It is not essential that the team members achieve total uniformity, but they should reach a consensus when making critical decisions. The team should define *consensus* as (1) all points of view have been heard and (2) the will of the group is evident even to those who oppose it (DuFour, 2001). Once the team has met these two conditions, the consensus choice will be evident. Move on it!

The Last Phase: Doing!

As a student of Richard DuFour, Robert Eaker, and Rebecca DuFour, I would often hear people ask them, "Where do we start?" An answer they often gave was to "get started and get better." The first edition of *Learning by Doing: A Handbook for Professional Learning Communities at Work* starts with the phrase, "We learn best by doing" (DuFour, DuFour, Eaker, & Many, 2006, p. 1). So the best way to improve your PLC practices is to commit to get started and get incrementally better. Celebrate your victories and learn from your mistakes.

In this pursuit to engage in the work and continuously improve, I include some tools in the appendix (page 145) to assist the guiding coalition and the school's staff in your journey.

- The *Time for Change* Decision-Making Guide for Building Consensus for Change (page 157) contains important characteristics for creating a loose-tight balance.

- The rubrics (pages 158, 160, 162, 164, 166, and 168) allow the guiding coalition to do a preassessment of each essential element of PLC Right. This information will help the team analyze specific deficiencies and make targeted, informed decisions about improving the PLC at Work process.

- The surveys (pages 159, 161, 163, 165, 167, and 169), which can be administered to staff, contain important questions about current perceptions of the six essential elements of PLC Right. These surveys will allow the guiding coalition to quantify philosophical trends and assess if shared learning or influence is necessary. If there is any doubt about how the staff perceive an aspect of the process, give the survey and analyze the results, and if necessary, plan to build shared knowledge to overcome their doubts.

Philosophical agreement with research on good educational practice will do little to improve student learning. Deep self-reflection on our application of that research provides a more effective route to improve student learning. As you use the tools in this book, do not look at them as mirrors for criticism. Instead, view them as road maps to action that can be universally taken to help more students succeed.

ESSENTIAL ELEMENT ONE

Educators work collaboratively rather than in isolation, take collective responsibility for student learning, and clarify the commitments they make to each other about how they will work together.

This first step in the PLC journey is, in essence, a cultural shift. In order to have an environment where changes in professional practice are implemented properly, the culture must nurture, not suppress, the technical strategies. The cultural foundation has to be built before the institution can stand the weight of change. This foundation must be built collaboratively and not just reflect the passion of one individual or a small group of individuals:

> Building shared knowledge about the current reality in the
> school as well as the research on the most promising practices
> in school improvement is a prerequisite for establishing the
> foundation of a PLC. Think of this foundation as resting on four
> pillars — (1) mission, (2) vision, (3) collective commitments, and
> (4) goals, each of which staff members understand and endorse.
> (DuFour & DuFour, 2012, p. 10)

To clarify the labor of foundation building, each essential element of building a philosophical commitment to the PLC at Work process can be described as collectively answering some essential questions.

1. **Mission:** Why do we exist?

2. **Vision:** What must we become in order to accomplish our fundamental purpose?

3. **Collective commitments:** How must we behave to create the school that will achieve this purpose?

4. **Goals:** How will we know if all of this is making a difference?

In my experience working directly with schools, I have found that this first stage of the PLC at Work process is generally skipped or poorly done. Schools and districts typically jump into the PLC work under the assumption that their culture is fundamentally aligned. But in many cases, their ideas about purpose, vision, behaviors, and indicators of success differ from those communicated by leadership. A school or school district that engages in the painstaking work of building philosophical consensus greatly increases its likelihood of succeeding in its PLC journey.

Adlai E. Stevenson High School in Lincolnshire, Illinois, is considered by many as the mother ship or incubator of the PLC process. Richard DuFour led this school for decades, and the school has earned its reputation as one of the best and most celebrated high schools in the United States. The work that Richard DuFour started in the 1980s with his staff, board of education, and community continues to pay off. Eric Twadell (2020), the current superintendent at Adlai E. Stevenson High School, asserts that clarity of purpose, future direction, collective commitments, and lofty goals are what sustain the school's success. I include the Adlai E. Stevenson High

School vision statement and collective commitments in the appendix (page 147). I encourage your guiding coalition to study this document and use it as a blueprint for building shared commitment.

To guide the work of building your school's cultural foundation, the guiding coalition might consider the following questions.

- How will we gather evidence of staff perceptions about student learning and the need to work together?

- What data should we gather to paint a profile of our current reality?

- What process should we use in developing collective commitments that are authentic and not ceremonial?

- What process should we use in setting critical school and team improvement goals? Who should be part of that process? How and how often will we monitor the process?

This first essential element may cause some discomfort, but the consensus that is gained is well worth it. Proceeding based on poor assumptions will lead to PLC Lite or another reboot five years down the road. Choose wisely.

ESSENTIAL ELEMENT TWO

The fundamental structure of the school becomes the collaborative team in which members work interdependently to achieve common goals for which all members are mutually accountable.

Clarity of purpose, direction, commitments, and goals provide us with a strong foundation. Now, we have to go to work. As established throughout this book, the research is clear that professionals who work together are much more effective and impactful than those who work alone. We have to accept that this shift is especially challenging for schools because we have a history of isolation and even of physical structures built around the concept of individualism. The platform that the PLC at Work process uses for collaboration and work is the collaborative team. These teams engage in the work of answering the four critical questions of a PLC.

The first important consideration regarding collaborative teams is team construction: the people who will work together. Making this determination can be a challenge, depending on the size and structure of the school. Earlier, I provided insights from Aaron Hansen (2015) and Brig Leane and Jon Yost (2022) on forming teams in small schools and for singleton teachers. A good question to consider when forming teams is, Who has the most learning outcomes in common (McLaughlin & Talbert, 2006)? If the focus of the team is improving student learning, student learning must be at the center of the team's collaboration.

The second critical consideration for collaborative teams is time. We are all painfully aware that time is always in short supply in schools. If learning is our primary objective, teachers need time to do the work demanded by the PLC at Work process. Not providing adequate time sends the message that PLC is not a priority:

> One of the ways in which organizations demonstrate their priorities is allocation of resources, and in schools, one of the most precious resources is time. Thus, school and district leaders must provide teachers with time to do the things they are being asked to do. (DuFour et al., 2016, p. 64)

I recommend that the guiding coalition reach out to Model PLC schools (see www .allthingsPLC.info) and consult the variety of literature available on creative ways to find collaborative time. From the analysis of the allocation of instructional versus collaborative time in Singapore compared to the United States, our issue with time is connected more to priority than to opportunity.

The third critical consideration is how teams will interact. We often call these commitments *team norms*. Team norms are not ambiguous descriptions of what each team hopes to do, but a specific and noticeable set of behaviors that every team member commits to doing to make the team experience pleasant and productive (Brown, Horn, & King, 2018). I recommend that the teams and guiding coalition revisit and analyze these commitments often.

The fourth critical consideration is how teams will be monitored. Micromanagement is never comfortable for the supervisor or those being supervised. People often ask me, "Who should run the PLC meetings—the principal or the teachers?" At its root, this question is about *power* instead of *functionality*. Ideally, the members of a team are so committed to their work and the goals of their work that they monitor themselves. In the worst-case scenario, the team is indifferent and disengaged and may need support from someone with more authority. Richard DuFour (2007) asks the question, "Does professional autonomy extend to the freedom to disregard what is widely considered best practice in one's field?" (p. 38). If we are truly committed to improving student learning, then the answer is *no*! The best way to monitor the work of teams is to require them to regularly submit products of their work: artifacts from their collective efforts to answer the four critical questions. This method will help the guiding coalition understand which teams are progressing at an acceptable rate and which teams may need some directive support.

The guiding coalition might consider the following questions to organize and focus its work toward building strong collaborative teams.

- How will we form our teams? Who must work together to improve student learning?

- Who are the educators who are difficult to place on a team (singletons), and what on-ramp would work best for them?

- How is our school day currently arranged, and what are the best pathways to find sacred, protected time for teachers to engage in the PLC work?

- What process will we use in leading teams to create norms? How often should teams review them? How will we respond if teams do not respect their norms and become dysfunctional?

- What products should we require from each team to analyze their progress on the PLC journey? Who among us will intervene if a team is not meeting our standards or expectations?

ESSENTIAL ELEMENT THREE

The team establishes a guaranteed and viable curriculum, unit by unit, so all students have access to the same knowledge and skills regardless of the teacher to whom they are assigned.

This task requires organization. Now we are getting into the weeds of the work, and technical practices are shifting significantly. Teachers have always analyzed curriculum and determined what is more important and less important based on their individual judgment. At this phase, individual choice in curricular priorities must take a back seat to collective choice. Aligning intended learning outcomes ensures that (1) students will not be penalized or rewarded based on the teachers to whom they are assigned, and (2) the definition of learning success will be clear to both the teacher and the student (Marzano, 2009b). These conditions are imperative in improving student learning.

The first critical consideration in establishing a guaranteed and viable curriculum is what curricular material and documents each team must have at its disposal to engage in the prioritization process. The process will probably run much more smoothly if the guiding coalition takes a lead role in gathering and distributing those documents. In chapter 4 (page 90), I provided a list of documents that should be considered when completing this task.

The second critical consideration is which protocol will best help teams choose the learning targets that are most essential. There are many protocols available for this task, and the guiding coalition should spend some time studying which protocol works best for their school or school district. I would recommend considering a protocol from professional development experts Larry Ainsworth and Kyra Donovan (2019) called *REAL*. This acronym helps team members separate their learning standards into *must-know* and *nice-to-know* categories. Their collaborative efforts will focus on the *must-know* standards.

- **Readiness for the next level of learning:** Standards that are essential to future learning

- **Endurance:** Standards that have utility beyond schooling—often called *life skills*

- **Alignment to high-stakes assessments:** Standards that are frequently tested externally

- **Leverage:** Standards that have connections to two or more curricular areas

Using this protocol, or a similar one, teams should have a framework for successfully completing this task.

The third critical consideration is what artifacts to gather and how to monitor team progress in this area. When I led this process, we required teams to use a standard document to identify their essential standards quarterly. Each department leader had to explain how each standard met the requirements of our protocol for choosing essential standards, and based on the collected documents, the guiding coalition either asked for clarity or approved the essential standards. To allow them to prepare for this requirement, the school gave each department (both core academics and electives) a full release day out of their classrooms each quarter, and provided substitute teachers for them.

In its pursuit of creating a guaranteed and viable curriculum, your guiding coalition might consider the following questions.

- What curricular material should we gather for teachers so they can make critical decisions about student learning outcomes?

- What protocol should we choose to guide the work of clarifying what's essential, and do our teachers need additional training or professional development to properly use our chosen protocol?

- Do our teachers need extended time, outside of their regularly scheduled meetings, to complete this task?

- How are we going to gather artifacts or evidence of each team's essential learning outcomes, and how are we going to vet and respond to the quality of those choices?

ESSENTIAL ELEMENT FOUR

The team develops common formative assessments to frequently gather evidence of student learning.

To commit to formative assessments is to declare that a school has left PLC Lite and is headed toward PLC Right. Richard DuFour and Robert Eaker would often refer to this practice as the *lynchpin of the process*—"one that serves to hold together parts or elements that exist or function as a unit" (Lynchpin, n.d.). In short, this practice holds all the parts of the PLC process together and creates interdependence. If there is one area that needs the passion of your guiding coalition, this is it. "Formative assessment works. That's right: Ample research evidence is now at hand to indicate emphatically that when the formative-assessment process is used, students learn better" (Popham, 2013).

In the previous chapter (page 43), I cited many scholars who have suggested reasons why we have not shifted from our traditional summative-only system to one that values formative assessment as well. The most common answer is quite simply that the shift is uncomfortable. When I reflect on my time as a classroom teacher, I am ashamed to think about my assessment practices. I definitely fit the mold of using assessments in a solely summative fashion. In their book *Instructional Agility: Responding to Assessment With Real-Time Decisions*, Cassandra Erkens, Tom Schimmer, and Nicole Dimich (2018) state:

> While teachers have always used assessment to judge student
> performance, classroom assessment in the 2000s and beyond
> has seen an infusion of assessment *for* learning—assessment not
> used to judge, grade, or score, but assessment to identify what
> comes next. (p. 3)

If a guiding coalition seeks to institutionalize formative assessment practices, it may want to start with analyzing current assessment practices and building some shared knowledge about how to develop and administer formative assessments. I have worked with hundreds of schools, and more often than not, teachers hesitate to deeply engage in formative assessment because of apprehension about their ability to do so effectively. In the *Time for Change* framework, this would be a *how* need.

The guiding coalition may also consider teachers' psychological safety related to repercussions for unfavorable student performance on a formative assessment. It would be wise for the school to produce a standard policy assuring teachers that their common formative assessment results will never be used to formally evaluate them (Many, 2006). There are many other indicators that a principal could gather if they wanted to make a case that a teacher is performing poorly and needs corrective action. The formative assessment process should be a sacred one used to improve teacher practice and strategically identify student learning needs.

Another important consideration of a guiding coalition is which tools and systems to use to collect, analyze, and utilize the data from common formative assessments. There are many modern technology tools that will allow your teams to collect and disaggregate data in ways that provide them with useful information. The guiding coalition should reach agreement about what systems would best meet the school's needs. Assessment experts Kim Bailey and Chris Jakicic (2023) have developed a simple but powerful team data-analysis protocol. They call the protocol *What? So What? Now What?*

- **What?:** What are the data telling us?

- **So what?:** What are our theories about why the data look as they do, and what does that tell us about our practice?

- **Now what?:** What are we going to do about what the data are telling us?

As with the other essential elements, the guiding coalition should decide how often to collect artifacts of a team's activity in developing and administering common formative assessments. Experience has taught us that simply assuming teams are engaged in this critical activity is beyond naive. The guiding coalition would be wise to follow a protocol for review and feedback. Since common formative assessments should never be used punitively, the guiding coalition's response to teams in need should be supportive. The only time that a leader would need to be directive or even punitive is when a team declares that it is not going to engage.

In their pursuit of universal engagement in the common formative assessment process, your guiding coalition might consider the following questions.

- What are our current assessment practices, and are they improving or hindering student growth?

- What is the assessment literacy of our staff? Do we need to invest in their professional capacity to improve our assessment practices?

- Do we have the right technology for assessment development, administration, and analysis of data?

- Do we have a protocol we could use as a standard for data analysis to increase the probability that the evidence will improve teacher practice and student learning?

- How are we going to collect artifacts from teams' formative assessment practices to provide support when necessary?

- Do we have a policy that shields teachers from punitive action if their formative assessment results don't favorably compare to their colleagues' results?

ESSENTIAL ELEMENT FIVE

The school has created a system of interventions and extensions to ensure students who struggle receive additional time and support for learning in a way that is timely, directive, diagnostic, and systematic, and students who demonstrate proficiency can extend their learning.

This element requires teams and the school to move from philosophy to action. Gathering evidence from the common formative assessments will give the teams valuable information, but information alone does not improve outcomes. That information has to be acted on. Historically, a teacher would conclude whether a student was capable upon their review of the student's assessment results. Looking at results through a totally summative lens can skew the educator's perception of the student's capacity and cause the educator to reach a false conclusion about the student's intelligence. The fact is that people learn in different ways and at different paces. A school truly committed to learning would have a systemic response, not individual responses, when students show a need for additional support or for extended learning on a particular standard.

I recommend that guiding coalition members educate themselves on good intervention systems. Read a book, attend a conference, or visit a school that is getting favorable results from their intervention systems. If there is one book that the guiding coalition has to read to properly engage in this effort, it is *Taking Action: A Handbook for RTI at Work* (Buffum, Mattos, & Malone, 2018). This book is thorough in its approach to proper student intervention, and a guiding coalition would greatly benefit from utilizing this resource in some way. The authors write:

> Because every student does not learn the same way or at the same speed, or enter school with the same prior access to learning, the school builds tiers of additional support to ensure every student's success. The school does not view these tiers as a pathway to traditional special education but instead as an ongoing process to dig deeper into students' individual needs. (Buffum et al., 2018, p. 19)

These authors suggest that the system of student support be broken into three tiers or levels of support (Buffum et al., 2018).

1. **Tier 1:** Access to essential grade-level standards for all students

2. **Tier 2:** Additional support to master grade-level standards

3. **Tier 3:** Intensive remediation in universal skills

Approaching this essential element using this framework will be powerful for teachers and students. Of all the elements of PLC Right, this one requires the most disruption to the status quo. Schedules may need to be rearranged, staff members may need to be assigned based on need instead of preference, and the system must move in real time.

In order to systematically meet the learning needs of all students, a guiding coalition should conduct a critical analysis of current needs and systems of response. Unfortunately, I witness many schools and school districts that leave student support on the shoulders of each individual classroom teacher instead of creating a system. The evidence shows that a driver of teacher anxiety is being stretched too thin. Intervention cannot be a solo act, and collaborative action in responding to student needs is more important now than ever before. Any school employees who are involved in the development of schedules, systems, or activities need to be considered in the alteration of time, structures, and systems. These employees might include teachers, counselors, instructional coaches, and paraprofessionals. There are many ways to intervene, but creating an intervention system that works for your school will require an all-hands-on-deck approach. Also, do not forget that part of this endeavor is to answer PLC critical question four and provide students with time to venture deeper into the essential curriculum. This reality often gets overlooked and poorly executed. Make it a priority.

The guiding coalition may also need to take an inventory of the staff's understanding of the intervention process and give them access to training and support to build their capacity. Simply giving students access to "intervention time" doesn't necessarily mean that something productive is taking place or that the students are making progress. Teachers and students must have time for intervention as well as utilize effective intervention strategies.

Finally, I would recommend that the guiding coalition consider how it is going to gather evidence of interventions' and extensions' effectiveness. What artifacts might the guiding coalition collect to monitor the impact of the intervention system? When I was a principal, my school tried many intervention strategies that did not yield much benefit, so we stopped doing them and tried something different. It was three years before I felt we had truly worked out all the critical bugs in our system. Only after this painful trial and error did I feel confident informing parents that school success for their children was imminent. This doesn't mean we waited three years to start; we started immediately, and we learned by doing!

A guiding coalition concerned about creating an airtight system of student support and extension might consider the following questions.

- Do we understand good intervention practices and systems, and how does our current system compare to best practice? Is our system multitiered and targeted to specific student needs?

- Do we need to invest in teacher capacity to build intervention skill? Are we looking at intervention and extension through an individual or collective lens?

- Whom do we need to gather to create a system that meets the needs of students at all the three tiers of support? Do we have the right people assigned within that system to meet student needs?

- How will we gather information to assess the effectiveness of our intervention system? How will we adjust in real time if there is a need for change?

- Have we considered critical question four and built in time for extended learning opportunities?

ESSENTIAL ELEMENT SIX

The team uses evidence of student learning to inform and improve the individual and collective practice of its members.

This last essential element is directly connected to the first one. If a school is serious about making student learning its fundamental purpose as an institution, then gathering and learning from the results of that effort seems obvious and logical. One of my mentors in the beginning of my school leadership career warned me to "never confuse activity for improvement." Unfortunately, schools do not always operate from this perspective. I cited Earl and Katz's (2006) work and research on data anxiety in the previous chapter (page 104). Results can be scary, especially when they are not favorable, and a school or district has to get comfortable with acting on brutal facts.

This commitment will require leadership to value school culture more than school climate. Leaders tend to value being liked, even if it interferes with essential business. Leadership's reluctance to create a data-driven culture has had the negative effect of improving school performance (Dhuey & Smith, 2014). Creating a data-driven culture requires leaders not to be unlikable but to place a premium on improving student learning, facing uncomfortable evidence, and focusing the professionals on the essential work that lies ahead.

Tim Kanold (2011), former superintendent at Adlai E. Stevenson High School, proclaims that a results orientation is what separates the PLC at Work process from other collaborative models. Many other collaborative models, like critical friends groups, encourage educators to discuss education topics, not the impact of their practice. PLC requires this constant self-analysis. The SMART goal process might be a valuable tool for a guiding coalition to consider in creating a results-driven culture. The acronym *SMART* stands for the following goal criteria (Conzemius & O'Neill, 2014).

- **S**trategic and specific
- **M**easurable
- **A**ttainable
- **R**esults oriented
- **T**ime bound

This process is a great protocol for schools and teams to set reasonable short-term goals. I also suggest that the guiding coalition consider using more ambitious, longer-term goals, often referred to as *stretch goals* (Tichy, 1997). Stretch goals challenge a team, school, or system to dream beyond what they believe is currently attainable. When I led the guiding coalition at Levey Middle School, we set a stretch goal to eliminate failing student grades through the effective use of our intervention system. It took four years, but we were able to achieve that milestone, and it sent positive shock waves throughout our community.

A guiding coalition charged with creating a data-driven or results-driven culture might consider differentiating between which data are important and which data are secondary.

- How much weight do we place on state testing compared to formative assessment?

- How will we measure and utilize nonacademic data, like attendance, discipline, and surveys collected by stakeholders?

- How will we use this evidence to make individual and collective decisions?

- Do we need to create a data protocol at all levels of the system? Should we utilize SMART goals? How and when should we create ambitious stretch goals?

Conclusion

This is the work of PLC Right! No task or practice is beyond every reader's school or district to accomplish. The tools at your disposal are endless. The guiding coalition work I laid out is doable, research-affirmed, and more critical today than ever before. When I started this journey in 2002, my staff and I did not have the tools that you have available today. Today, you have the following resources.

- **AllThingsPLC website**
  (www.allthingsplc.info)

- *AllThingsPLC Magazine*
  (professional learning community articles; www.solutiontree.com /all-things-plc-magazine.html)

- **Hundreds of PLC at Work–themed books and videos**
  (www.solutiontree.com/products.html?topics=5493)

- **Live on-site PLC at Work events**
  (Institutes; www.solutiontree.com/events/on-site-events.html
  ?eventtype=5567&topics=5493)

- **Virtual and technology-based tools**
  (Global PD Teams; www.solutiontree.com/globalpdteams)

When I led the PLC at Work process, all that my staff and I had at our disposal were the first PLC book (DuFour & Eaker, 1998), a guiding coalition, and a strong desire. Who knows what we could have accomplished if we had all the tools that the modern educator has available to get really good at this process. I am comfortable saying that if a school today can't properly utilize this process to improve student learning or it settles for PLC Lite, it's because that school doesn't want PLC Right bad enough and improving student learning is not its passion.

Pause to Think and Plan

Amen!

_____

_____

_____

_____

_____

Aha!

_____

_____

_____

_____

_____

So What?

_____

_____

_____

_____

_____

_____

Afterword

I hope this book challenged you. My goal as an author and educational consultant is to stretch people, but never to injure them. I felt compelled to address some touchy topics in an effort to push readers to self-reflect. The future is in our hands. We can choose to give in to the moment or act with a sense of urgency to build something better for the generations that follow us. We certainly are all beneficiaries of the sacrifices of those who came before us, and I would like to know that future generations will be equally grateful for our contributions.

In this afterword, I would like to speak directly to several groups of people.

To government officials: I beg you to abandon divisive partisan politics and populism. History has shown those always have tragic ends. McCarthyism of the 1940s didn't end well, and history casts an unfavorable shadow over those who participated. Marginalizing people through policy doesn't move us closer to our goal of *liberty and justice for all*. Do you still believe in these founding principles? You can use your power for the common good instead of division. In 2018, Richard DuFour, Douglas Reeves, and Rebecca DuFour released a book titled *Responding to the Every Student Succeeds Act With the PLC at Work Process.* This book goes into great detail about how politicians and governments can use the power of the federal law known as the Every Student Succeeds Act (ESSA), which was passed in 2015 to replace the No Child Left Behind Act, to promote student improvement through the PLC at Work process. ESSA differs from NCLB because it places the weight of structuring school-improvement policies and systems at the state level, as opposed to the federal level under NCLB.

I remember sitting down with a group of legislators from the state of Arkansas after a PLC Institute in Atlanta, Georgia. The members included individuals from the education committees of both houses of Congress, along with the state education secretary, Johnny Key. Like other states, Arkansas was considering how to structure its system to respond to the new ESSA law. The conversation went on for hours and stayed focused on the best pathway forward for schools and students in the state of Arkansas. I could not tell which legislators were Republicans, Democrats, or Independents. Their party affiliations were not evident, but their sincere vigor for supporting Arkansas students was clear.

Arkansas decided to be a pioneer in the statewide implementation of PLC at Work, and the results have been phenomenal. A 2023 editorial published in *The New York Times* revealed that the Arkansas PLC project has involved over one hundred schools, and the participating schools have experienced 31 percent less COVID-19-related learning loss, fewer student discipline issues, and drastically lower teacher turnover than other schools in the state (Key & Eaker, 2023). Their success has also been documented by an independent research laboratory, Education Northwest. I would encourage legislators and state education officials to reach out to the Arkansas Department of Education so they can review the documented improvements from a statewide effort to make the PLC at Work process the norm in schools.

To school leaders: You sit in a powerful position. You can either accelerate your journey toward greatness or sabotage that journey by diverting your attention to topics that don't advance student learning success. I spent almost a decade as a classroom teacher, but I had the most impact on the lives of students as a school leader who could inspire high expectations and good practice throughout my entire school, not just in one classroom.

When I was a graduate student, a professor asked me to speak with him after class. I was a little shocked by his request, but I complied. Once we were alone, he told me that he thought I had a lot of potential as a leader, but he wanted me to remember his words of advice: Leadership is about making decisive decisions for the greater good of the organization. It is not a popularity contest. You will always offend someone when you make an impactful decision; just be certain that you can live with the response of the party you offend.

Those words have impacted my behavior as a leader since that important encounter. I made up my mind that the only party I cannot live with offending are *students*. In this era of culture wars, political bickering, and conflicting ideologies in our society, have the courage to make decisions that strengthen students but sometimes disappoint adults. Create a guiding coalition and share leadership. Organize your school into teacher teams and focus on the four critical PLC at Work questions. These are the practices and decisions that lead to student success. We need you to be strong and resolute in your commitment to PLC at Work. Like my professor told me, leadership is not a popularity contest.

To practitioners: You work on the front line. We need you to advocate for our profession. Thousands of educators attend PLC events every year, yet we do not witness enough schools trending in the direction of PLC Right. The destiny of our profession is in your hands. Activists came before you, but the age of activism is not over. We must demand a living wage for teachers. We must demand that schools provide teachers with adequate collaborative time and equip them with the tools to properly implement PLC at Work. Don't wait on someone else to advocate for our profession and for our children; we have to be advocates. I am counting on you to help me keep my promise to Rick DuFour.

Appendix

The first policy in the board policy manual of Adlai E. Stevenson High School District 125 articulates the vision of the school the district is attempting to create. Each constituency then articulates the collective commitments its members have made to bring this vision to life.

Adlai E. Stevenson High School Vision Statement

Stevenson High School is an exemplary learning community school. To ensure future development and growth, the school must have a clear sense of the goals it is trying to accomplish, the characteristics of the school it seeks to become, and the contributions the various stakeholders in the school will make in order to transform ideals into reality. The following vision statement is intended to provide the standards Stevenson High School should strive to achieve and maintain.

1. **Curriculum, Instruction, and Assessment**

   An exemplary learning community provides students with a common coherent curriculum complemented with a variety of elective courses and cocurricular activities. This balanced program stimulates intellectual curiosity, requires students to demonstrate they have learned how to learn, and leads students to develop into productive and responsible citizens. The school articulates the outcomes it seeks for all its students and monitors and assesses each student's attainment of those outcomes through a variety of indicators. In such a school:

   a. The curriculum addresses important academic content and essential life skills

   b. The curriculum broadens each student's perspective in order to understand and appreciate diversity

   c. Instructional strategies reflect best practice and stimulate student engagement

   d. Instructional practice promotes and integrates appropriate technology to enhance curricular outcomes and cocurricular pursuits

   e. Assessment is an ongoing practice containing both formative and summative components

   f. Assessment is used to ensure quality learning and to inform teachers and teams regarding curricular and instructional decision making

   g. Curriculum, instructional practice, and assessment recognize and accommodate individual differences, interests, and abilities

   h. Curriculum, instructional practice, and assessment reflect the district's support of innovation and commitment to continuous improvement

2. **Emphasis on the Individual Student: Equity and Access for *All***

   An exemplary learning community recognizes and values the importance of the individual student. Staff members are committed to understanding the uniqueness of each student. In the final analysis, the effectiveness of any school is based on the conduct, character, and achievement of its students. In an exemplary learning community, these qualities are a result of genuine concern for the individual student. In such a school:

a. Each student will be provided the information, assistance, and support to develop appropriate educational and career goals for transitioning to and through high school

b. Attention will be paid to the whole student, including academic progress, behavior, and emotional well-being, with the initiation of appropriate services as needed

c. Staff will facilitate students' development of the skills necessary to become independent, lifelong learners

d. Staff will guide students in accepting increasing responsibility for their learning, decisions, and actions

e. Each student will be encouraged to explore and take advantage of the variety of opportunities for participation in the curricular and cocurricular programs

f. Students will fulfill the expectation to be actively engaged and give their best efforts, intellectually and ethically, to their academic and cocurricular pursuits

g. All members of the Stevenson learning community will conduct themselves in a way that contributes to a safe and orderly environment that respects the rights of others within a diverse community

3. **Work Within a Professional Learning Community**

    An exemplary learning community operates on the premise that success for every student is dependent on the people in the organization. Therefore, the board, administration, and staff are committed to recruiting, developing, and retaining individuals with exceptional expertise in their respective fields and a passionate commitment to the school as a professional learning community. In such a school, the board, administration, and staff:

    a. Actively promote and honor the district's vision, values, and goals

    b. Have high standards and expectations for student success and engage in reflection and collective inquiry regarding best practices

c. Are committed to contributing to high-performing collaborative teams

d. Model the importance of lifelong learning through a commitment to ongoing professional development

e. Are committed to collective inquiry and reflection on the results of student achievement in order to improve student learning

f. Are committed to a high level of mutual support and trust among all members of the learning community

4. **A Culture for Learning**

An exemplary learning community creates a safe, caring environment and fosters a culture that promotes collaboration, enables staff and students to explore their full learning potentials, and results in meaningful learning experiences. This culture contributes to a shared sense of pride in the school. In such a school:

a. There is a commitment to maintain an emotionally and physically safe, supportive environment

b. Well-maintained physical facilities meet the needs of all members of the Stevenson community and reflect pride in the school

c. There is an ongoing effort to provide a school that is free of alcohol, other drugs, and violence

d. The diverse community of students and staff treats each other with mutual respect, consideration, and acceptance

e. There is open and ongoing communication among all members of the Stevenson community

f. Staff and students are encouraged to participate in curricular and cocurricular challenges in order to promote personal growth

g. Individual and collective efforts and achievements are promoted, recognized, and celebrated

h. Learning is recognized as dynamic and socially constructed, requiring student engagement, collaboration, and supportive relationships with one's peers and teachers

5. **Community Engagement**

An exemplary learning community values the importance of collaborative relationships with its extended community—families, residents, businesses, government agencies, and other educational systems. It strives to develop a strong commitment between the community and the school. In such a school:

a. The extended community shares and promotes the vision and values of the school

b. The extended community provides the various resources that enable the school to offer exemplary academic and cocurricular programs and expects effective stewardship of those resources

c. The community and the school value and recognize the mutual benefit of exchanging information and feedback

d. The community is encouraged to utilize school resources and facilities

e. Parents play an active role in the education of their children, monitor their children's academic performance, and work collaboratively and positively with staff to maximize their children's educational experience

f. The school, the business community, and other organizations collaborate to provide authentic learning experiences for students and staff, thereby reinforcing the relevance of the academic and cocurricular programs

g. The school continually seeks effective partnerships with sender districts and institutions of higher education

h. The school serves as a lighthouse, interacting and collaborating with the educational community at large

i. The school provides opportunities for students to serve and participate within the extended community

Stevenson High School Board and Administrative Leadership Team Collective Commitments

The board and administrative leadership team of Stevenson High School are committed to the education and well-being of each student. As part of a professional learning community, we have identified the following values in order to guide the policies, procedures, programs, priorities, and day-to-day decisions of the district. The team will honor, advance, and protect these values. We will also acknowledge and address behaviors that are inconsistent with the district's vision and goals.

- We will model and advance the behaviors established in the Stevenson vision statement to all members of the Stevenson community. These behaviors include:

  - Active promotion of the district's vision, values, and goals

  - High standards and expectations for student success and engagement in reflection and collective inquiry regarding best practices

  - A commitment to the contribution toward high-performing collaborative teams

  - A commitment to lifelong learning through ongoing professional development and growth

  - A commitment to collective inquiry and reflection on the results of student achievement in order to improve student learning

  - A commitment to a high level of mutual support and trust among all members of the learning community

- We will recruit and retain individuals who are best suited to advance the vision and goals of the district, and we will create conditions that support their ongoing professional growth.

- We will facilitate the development of curricular and cocurricular programs that result in high levels of student engagement, address student needs and interests, integrate technology when appropriate for achieving program goals, and enable students to understand and appreciate diversity.

- We will model, monitor, and enforce student and adult behaviors that contribute to a safe and orderly environment while respecting the rights of others within a diverse community.

- We will develop and implement policies, programs, and procedures to monitor and support collective achievement and individual student success.

- We will develop and implement policies, programs, and procedures that result in increased responsibility for student learning, decisions, and actions.

- We will recognize and celebrate the individual and collective efforts and achievements of the Stevenson community.

- We will fulfill our responsibilities for good stewardship by managing the district's resources in a manner that addresses the needs of the community, establishes community partnerships, and builds community support.

- We will fulfill our responsibilities as leaders of a lighthouse school, providing effective interaction and collaboration with the educational community at large.

These commitments are designed to help the board and administrative leadership team serve the advancement of the five components of the vision document: (1) Curriculum, Instruction, and Assessment; (2) Emphasis on the Individual Student: Equity and Access for All; (3) Work Within a Professional Learning Community; (4) a Culture for Learning; and (5) Community Engagement.

Stevenson High School Faculty Collective Commitments

We have established these guiding principles as a basis for our values as teachers and professionals at Stevenson High School. They are intended as a means for informal personal reflection and are not intended to be used in the formal evaluation process. They represent our shared purpose and will continue to guide us as educators.

- We will develop curriculum and instructional strategies that utilize various resources, which will promote the active involvement of students and provide for their varied experiences as well as their individual abilities and talents.

- We will assist each student in their transition into high school, through high school, and beyond by providing appropriate instruction, monitoring their progress, and offering guidance and support services tailored to individual needs.

- We will model the importance of lifelong learning through our ongoing professional development.

- We will collaborate with one another to create conditions that provide equity and promote student success.

- We will act in a professional manner with integrity and honesty and develop relationships characterized by care and respect—relationships that will lead to a rewarding professional experience.

- We will provide a supportive school atmosphere where everyone feels emotionally, physically, and intellectually safe.

- We will hold high expectations for student achievement and character, and will guide students to make responsible choices for their lives and the learning process.

- We will care for our physical environment and school property and will expect the same of students.

- We will communicate with parents and each other about students and encourage parents to be positively involved in their children's education.

Stevenson High School Support Staff Collective Commitments

As members of the Stevenson High School support staff, we affirm our active participation in helping Stevenson achieve its mission to become an exemplary learning community. In fulfilling our respective responsibilities, we share the following common commitments.

- We will support the collective effort to create the school described in Stevenson's vision document.

- We will foster a safe, nurturing, responsible, and positive environment that is conducive to the academic, ethical, and social growth of each individual student.

- We will continue to develop and support positive relationships with our colleagues, students, and community.

- We will show appreciation for cultural diversity and be sensitive to the thoughts and opinions of others.

- We will participate in effective and open communication throughout the school and community.

- We will pursue a commitment to continuous improvement in our performance.

- We will honor our commitment to lifelong learning.

- We will demonstrate pride and ownership in the school taking responsibility for informed decision making.

- We will develop a sense of responsibility and mutual respect in each student.

- We will celebrate school accomplishments and promote school spirit.

Collective Commitments for Stevenson Students

For more than thirty years, Stevenson High School has been building a tradition of excellence. As a student of Stevenson, you are asked to help contribute to that tradition. By maintaining high personal expectations for success, utilizing open communication with staff and fellow students, and following the guidelines listed here, you both increase your opportunities for success and help make Stevenson an excellent school.

To ensure this success, we will:

- Take responsibility for our education, decisions, and actions

- Act in a manner that best represents ourselves, our school, and our community

- Be active in the school and community

- Maintain a balance between academics, cocurricular activities, and other endeavors, continually giving our best efforts to each

- Respect our fellow students and their activities

- Respect cultural diversity, individuality, and the choices and rights of others

- Promote a safe and healthy learning environment

Collective Commitments for Stevenson Parents

We, as parents, must first become familiar with the established vision statement of Stevenson High School. We can contribute to the pursuit of that vision and the success of our children when we do the following.

1. Become informed and knowledgeable about the curricular, cocurricular, and student support programs available to students by:

   ‣ Carefully reviewing school publications such as the curriculum coursebook, cocurricular handbook, and student guidebook

   ‣ Attending and participating in parent information programs sponsored by the school

   ‣ Reading *The Minuteman* each month

   ‣ Reading or using the Stevenson website

2. Assist our children in making important educational decisions by:

   ‣ Helping them set educational goals that are appropriate to their individual capabilities, interests, and needs

   ‣ Participating in the course selection process

   ‣ Encouraging involvement in school activities

   ‣ Helping our children identify and pursue postsecondary education and career goals

3. Engage in open and timely communication with the school by:

   ‣ Responding to the school's feedback about our children's academic progress and behavior

▸ Advising school personnel of any special circumstances or needs of our children

▸ Being proactive in asking questions, expressing concerns, and seeking information

4. Become actively involved in the life of the school by:

▸ Attending school programs

▸ Participating in parent support groups such as the Patriot Parent Association, booster clubs, task forces, and so on

▸ Volunteering in the school

▸ Acting as advocates for quality education within the community

▸ Utilizing the resources of the school through adult education and community access programs

▸ Promoting Stevenson to the extended community

5. Help our children become responsible, self-reliant members of the school community by:

▸ Teaching them to accept responsibility for their own learning, decisions, and behavior

▸ Insisting they observe the rules of the school

▸ Demonstrating respect, consideration, and cooperation in dealing with others, and expecting our children to do the same

6. Create a supportive environment for learning in our homes by:

▸ Modeling the importance of lifelong learning

▸ Providing a quiet time and place for study

▸ Helping our children make connections between their learning experiences and their everyday lives

▸ Expecting achievement and offering encouragement and praise

7. Promote healthy lifestyles by:

▸ Modeling and supporting responsible lifestyle choices

▸ Monitoring the activities of our children and responding to behavior that jeopardizes their health and well-being

- ▸ Becoming informed of the risks associated with teenage use of alcohol, tobacco, and other drugs

- ▸ Discussing and developing family rules that prohibit illegal use of alcohol, tobacco, and other drugs

Time for Change Decision-Making Guide for Building Consensus for Change

(Why?) **Communication**	• All stakeholders have been provided with relevant data. • The rationale for change has been thoroughly explained by leadership. • Several viable alternatives have been explored, and all points of view have been heard.
(Who?) **Trust Building**	• Past unpleasant experiences of change have been heard and acknowledged. • A safe platform has been established for different points of view to be shared without fear of repercussions. • All parties are willing to place the student's best interests at the forefront of their decisions.
(How?) **Capacity Building**	• Prior knowledge has been assessed, and a plan to build shared knowledge has been created. • Our professional growth activities are primarily focused on building our capacity for practices essential to our needs. • Resources have been established to provide educators with assistance if they struggle.
(Do!) **Accountability**	• A system of accountability for implementation has been established, and it includes the collection and analysis of artifacts of the work. • Expectations for implementation and performance have been established, and they are clear and applied fairly to everyone.

Time for Change Framework for Building Consensus

Characteristic One	4 Exemplary Level of Development and Implementation	3 Fully Functional and Operational Level of Development and Implementation	2 Limited Development or Partial Implementation	1 Little to No Development and Implementation
Educators work collaboratively rather than in isolation, take collective responsibility for student learning, and clarify the commitments they make to each other about how they will work together. Items for review: • Master schedule • Academic assessment data • Attendance and discipline data • Survey data • School-improvement plan • Collective bargaining agreement • Artifacts from the collaborative process	Student learning drives every system in our school. All faculty members are aware of our passion for student learning, and professional dialogue centers on student learning. We collaborate at every level of our school. Teachers work on strong teams with a collective focus on student learning, and we regularly produce evidence of our work. We set student learning improvement goals at the team and school levels. We revisit our progress on a regular basis, and we are making phenomenal progress. We report our progress to all our essential stakeholders.	Student learning is important in our school and is the general topic of collaborative dialogue both formally and informally. We are given adequate time to collaborate, and most of our teams focus on student learning and take collective responsibility for student success. We set student learning improvement goals at the team and school levels. We regularly revisit our progress on our goals, and we are making incremental progress.	Student learning is mentioned often in our environment, but only as it relates to state test scores and school accountability rankings. We are given time to collaborate, but most teams have not achieved interdependence in their focus on collective student success. We set improvement goals on state assessment scores only, and they are only reviewed regularly if the school is in danger of an unfavorable accountability rating by the state.	We are generally aware that student learning is sporadic, but we do not have a strategic plan to improve. Each teacher makes independent decisions about student learning and is solely responsible for student success. We do not set improvement goals, or goals are set and most staff members are unaware of their existence, and we never reflect on our progress.

page 1 of 12

The Way Forward © 2024 Solution Tree Press • SolutionTree.com
Visit **go.SolutionTree.com/PLCbooks** to download this free reproducible.

Survey for Assessing Collective Commitments to Student Learning

1: Strongly Disagree	2: Disagree	3: Neutral	4: Agree			5: Strongly Agree	
			1	2	3	4	5
I believe that student learning should be the primary focus of our school and that educators are most responsible in that pursuit.							
I believe that student learning improves when teachers work together and pursue that goal collectively.							
I believe that we have an obligation to reflect on our professional practice and make adjustments based on student learning.							
The faculty have an obligation to create a collaborative vision for improvement and monitor their own progress.							
We have an obligation to collaboratively create a professional code of ethics and professional commitments that are universally embraced and monitored.							
We should set specific improvement goals and regularly monitor our own progress.							
We have an obligation to learn together, and our professional learning should be aligned with our vision.							
We should gather the input of critical stakeholders like parents, students, and the community when creating a vision for the future.							
We should collaborate with the central office and the board of education in creating and pursuing our vision.							
We should not vent frustration and disdain for others with colleagues because it is unprofessional and it undermines our progress toward our vision.							

page 2 of 12

Characteristic Two	**4** Exemplary Level of Development and Implementation	**3** Fully Functional and Operational Level of Development and Implementation	**2** Limited Development or Partial Implementation	**1** Little to No Development and Implementation
The fundamental structure of the school becomes the collaborative team in which members work interdependently to achieve common goals for which all members are mutually accountable. Items for review: • School budget • School staffing allocation • Master schedule • Team products • Collective bargaining agreement • School district and board policies	Teachers are organized into teams and have enough time to collaborate, and we value our teams. We have strong evidence that teaming improves teacher practice, and we regularly review our practices and engage in collective inquiry to improve our practices and team function. We view student learning as a collaborative task that lies heavily on the shoulders of professionals collaborating on a strong team. We have witnessed exemplary growth in student learning outcomes, and we can trace that improvement back to our collaborative efforts.	Teachers are organized into teams and have enough time to collaborate, and we value our teams. We agree that teaming can improve teacher practice, and we are making consistent strides in improving our team function and our practices. We view student learning as a collaborative task that lies heavily on the shoulders of professionals collaborating on a strong team. We are witnessing promising growth in student learning outcomes, and we can trace that improvement back to our collaborative efforts.	Teachers are currently organized into teams, but the structure is inadequate, and many view time spent with teams as a waste of time. We agree that teaming can improve teacher practice, but not in our current format or within our current culture. We view student learning as the individual responsibility of the teacher, student, or parent. We are open to the possibility of collaborative impact within the right structure and culture.	We do not currently organize teachers into teams. We do not currently agree that working on teams improves our practice, and we prefer to work in isolation. We view student learning as the individual responsibility of the teacher, student, or parent.

page 3 of 12

Survey for Assessing Collaborative Teams

1: Strongly Disagree 2: Disagree 3: Neutral 4: Agree 5: Strongly Agree	1	2	3	4	5
I believe that I have been placed on a productive team with the right members.					
My team is clear on our purpose, and we use our time to achieve our objectives.					
The time that I spend with my team is valuable, it is productive, and it improves my practice.					
My team has enough time to collaborate.					
Our work as a team is clearly defined.					
My team has enough resources to adequately engage in our work.					
My team has established reasonable norms, and we honor those norms.					
My team regularly analyzes student learning data.					
My team sets measurable goals on student learning, and we take collective responsibility for meeting those goals.					
Our school leadership supports collaborative teams and monitors our progress.					

page 4 of 12

Characteristic Three	**4** Exemplary Level of Development and Implementation	**3** Fully Functional and Operational Level of Development and Implementation	**2** Limited Development or Partial Implementation	**1** Little to No Development and Implementation
The team establishes a guaranteed and viable curriculum, unit by unit, so all students have access to the same knowledge and skills regardless of the teacher to whom they are assigned. Items for review: • State academic standards • District academic standards • Exploratory studies and electives standards • Social-emotional learning documents • Curricular material, including textbooks and online learning resources • Local, district, or state testing data • Collective bargaining agreement	We understand and agree about the necessity of selecting essential learning outcomes that are aligned course by course and unit by unit, and we make that information available to all stakeholders. In cooperation with our school or district leadership, we have collaboratively adopted a standard-prioritization protocol that is research based and applied across our entire school. We are given time to review, vet, and analyze curricular standards until we reach a consensus about what is essential, and we use data to monitor impact.	We understand and agree about the necessity of selecting essential learning outcomes that are aligned course by course and unit by unit. In cooperation with our school or district leadership, we have collaboratively adopted a standard-prioritization protocol that is research based and applied across our entire school. We are given time to review, vet, and analyze curricular standards until we reach a consensus about what is essential, but we do not use data to monitor impact.	We do not find it necessary to reach a consensus about essential learning outcomes. Our school or district leadership fully controls the selection of essential learning outcomes. We do not have a protocol to differentiate essential from nonessential learning outcomes. School or district leadership chooses them for us. Our school does not allocate time for teachers to review, analyze, and reach a consensus about essential learning outcomes. Time is allocated for school or district officials to inform us of their choices.	We do not find it necessary to reach a consensus about essential learning outcomes. All curricular decisions are left up to individual classroom teachers. We do not have a protocol to differentiate essential from nonessential learning outcomes. Our school does not allocate time for teachers to review, analyze, and reach a consensus about essential learning outcomes.

Survey for Checking for a Guaranteed and Viable Curriculum

1: Strongly Disagree 2: Disagree 3: Neutral	4: Agree		5: Strongly Agree		
	1	2	3	4	5
We believe that identifying essential learning outcomes is important to improving student learning.					
We are given time to collaboratively agree on curricular priorities and align essential learning outcomes.					
We collaborate with our school and district administration in coordinating a process to identify and align essential learning outcomes.					
We have adopted a protocol for prioritizing curriculum that is respected and universally applied.					
We have received adequate training on the process of choosing essential learning outcomes.					
We share our essential learning outcomes with students and parents.					
Our leadership reviews and provides feedback about our essential learning outcomes.					
Our collaborative team time is focused on the essential learning outcomes.					
We periodically review and make changes to our essential learning outcomes.					
Our assessments are aligned with our essential learning outcomes.					

page 6 of 12

Characteristic Four	4 Exemplary Level of Development and Implementation	3 Fully Functional and Operational Level of Development and Implementation	2 Limited Development or Partial Implementation	1 Little to No Development and Implementation
The team develops common formative assessments to frequently gather evidence of student learning. Items for review: • Essential standards documents • Summative assessment data (school, district, and state) • Assessment exemplars from curricular resources (like unit tests) • Collective bargaining agreement	We universally embrace the idea of formative assessment as a tool to improve student learning, and both teachers and students are engaged. All teams deeply integrate common formative assessment into their collaboration and professional practice, and teams are improving. All our teams use their collaborative time to analyze the impact of their practice and identify students for additional support. They also implement strategies that involve students in reflection on their own learning.	We universally embrace the idea of formative assessment as a tool to improve student learning. All teams integrate common formative assessment into their collaboration and professional practice, but some teams are much more effective than others. All our teams use their collaborative time to analyze the impact of their practice and identify students for additional support. Some teams are much more effective than others.	We do not universally embrace the idea of formative assessment. The staff are ideologically split. Some teams develop policies or protocols that integrate the use of formative assessment in their collaboration and professional practice. Some teams use their collaborative time to analyze the impact of their practice and identify students for additional support. Some use that time to determine which students are capable or incapable of learning.	We do not embrace the idea of formative assessment. Students either pass or fail. We do not have a policy or protocol that demands the use of formative assessment in our professional practice. We spend our collaborative time discussing summative assessment data to determine which students are capable and which are incapable of learning.

Survey for Assessing Common Formative Assessments

1: Strongly Disagree 2: Disagree 3: Neutral 4: Agree 5: Strongly Agree					
	1	2	3	4	5
Our staff clearly understand the difference between formative assessment and summative assessment.					
Teams use essential learning outcomes to develop common formative assessments.					
Teams use the evidence from common formative assessments to reflect on the impact of their own practice.					
Teams use common formative assessments to identify effective strategies and learn from one another.					
Common formative assessments are never used to evaluate a teacher or describe a teacher's quality.					
Evidence from common formative assessments is shared with students for self-reflection without sanction or punishment.					
We do not use evidence from common formative assessments to draw conclusions about student intelligence in general.					
We have policies or protocols that guide teams on the development and use of common formative assessments.					
We act on the evidence gathered from common formative assessments in a timely fashion.					

Characteristic Five	**4** Exemplary Level of Development and Implementation	**3** Fully Functional and Operational Level of Development and Implementation	**2** Limited Development or Partial Implementation	**1** Little to No Development and Implementation
The school has created a system of interventions and extensions to ensure students who struggle receive additional time and support for learning in a way that is timely, directive, diagnostic, and systematic, and students who demonstrate proficiency can extend their learning. Items for review: • Formative and summative assessment data • Master schedule • Staffing or full-time equivalent allocation • Staff professional certification information • Budget documents • Collective bargaining agreement	All teachers or teams participate in a schoolwide system of student interventions, and our positive impact is measurable and predictable. We set aside time for student academic and behavioral support. The support is directive and tailored to individual student needs. We allocate time for student extension as well, and it is an equal priority. We collect data and analyze and monitor student academic and behavioral progress. Our data reveal that our efforts are improving indicators of student learning, and proficient students are moving toward mastery.	All teachers or teams participate in a schoolwide system of student interventions, but effectiveness varies. We set aside time for student academic and behavioral support. The support is directive, but the strategies used are not always targeted to individual student needs. We allocate time for student extension as well, but it is not a top priority. We collect data and analyze and monitor student academic and behavioral progress. Our data reveal that our efforts are improving indicators of student learning.	Some teachers or teams collaboratively act when students do not meet performance expectations. We set aside time for student academic and behavioral support, but the support is not targeted or directive. We collect data and analyze and monitor student academic and behavioral progress. But we do not have any institutionalized standards or norms on how we will respond to that evidence.	We do not collectively act when a student does not meet performance expectations. That is the choice of the individual teacher. We do not have time set aside to respond to student needs in a way that is timely and directive. We do not collect data, nor do we analyze or monitor student academic and behavioral progress.

page 9 of 12

The Way Forward © 2024 Solution Tree Press • SolutionTree.com
Visit **go.SolutionTree.com/PLCbooks** to download this free reproducible.

Survey for Assessing Interventions and Extensions

1: Strongly Disagree 2: Disagree 3: Neutral	4: Agree		5: Strongly Agree		
	1	2	3	4	5
We believe that it is our responsibility to act when a student does not meet our learning expectations.					
We believe that student support should be mandatory, not invitational, when a student does not meet our learning expectations.					
We have adequate time built into our school day to provide students with targeted support.					
Our school collaborates to meet students' needs; meeting their needs is not solely the responsibility of each teacher.					
Our leadership provides us with enough resources to meet the needs of students who need extra time and support.					
Intervention time is used wisely, and our staff feel confident in our intervention practices.					
Our leadership monitors the impact and effectiveness of our intervention procedures.					
We provide proficient students with an opportunity to extend their understanding of essential curriculum.					
Student extension and personalized learning are priorities at our school.					
Students are able to monitor their progress and are invested in their own growth.					

page 10 of 12

Characteristic Six	4 Exemplary Level of Development and Implementation	3 Fully Functional and Operational Level of Development and Implementation	2 Limited Development or Partial Implementation	1 Little to No Development and Implementation
The team uses evidence of student learning to inform and improve the individual and collective practice of its members. Items for review: • Formative and summative assessment data • Professional development plans • School-improvement plan • Collective bargaining agreement	We collect evidence of student learning, and it is the primary focus of our collaborative meetings. We use that evidence to improve practice at the classroom and school levels. Our leadership collects artifacts from teams of teachers and monitors data at a macro level to improve team and schoolwide practice. All our conversations at the team and school levels are evidence based. We create SMART goals at the team and school levels to monitor our progress.	We collect evidence of student learning, and it is the primary focus of our collaborative meetings. We learn from one another regularly, but do not monitor our adjustments to our practice. Our leadership collects artifacts of our collaborative practice and provides valuable insight for improvement. We frequently have moments of reflection during our collaborative time, and teams create SMART goals to monitor our progress.	We collect evidence of student learning, and we have interesting discussions, but rarely act. Our leadership has created a superficial monitoring document for our team, and we complete it as an act of compliance. We occasionally have moments of reflection during our collaborative time on ways to improve our practice, but these instances are infrequent. We spend most of our time critiquing the behaviors of others.	We use our collaborative time to discuss topics of interest to the members, not evidence of student learning. Our leadership does not monitor our collaboration and takes little interest in our interactions. We use collaborative time to critique the behaviors of others (students, administration, parents, society at large, and so on).

Survey for Assessing Perceptions of a Results Orientation

1: Strongly Disagree	2: Disagree	3: Neutral	4: Agree		5: Strongly Agree		
			1	**2**	**3**	**4**	**5**
We view objective evidence as valid and reliable.							
We believe that data help improve our individual and collective practice.							
Our decisions are research and evidence based.							
I feel safe learning from my teammates if they produce better results than I do.							
Our leadership uses results to help guide us at the team and school levels.							
Our teams create SMART goals that guide our work and allow us to assess the impact of our work.							
Results are used not to compare people in our school, but to identify promising practices.							
Results are used as learning tools and not used to compare one person or team against another.							
We are celebrated when we achieve promising or good results.							
We use results to celebrate and motivate students.							

page 12 of 12

References
and Resources

Academic support. (2013, August 29). In *The glossary of education reform*. Accessed at www.edglossary.org/academic-support on July 12, 2023.

Achievement gap. (2013, December 19). In *The glossary of education reform*. Accessed at www.edglossary.org/achievement-gap on July 12, 2023.

Ainsworth, L., & Donovan, K. (2019). *Rigorous curriculum design: How to create curricular units of study that align standards, instruction, and assessment* (2nd ed.). Rexford, NY: International Center for Leadership in Education.

Aldeman, C. (2022, September 28). Why are fewer people becoming teachers? [Blog post]. *Education Next*. Accessed at www.educationnext.org/why-are-fewer-people-becoming-teachers on July 12, 2023.

Almukhtar, S., Lai, K. K. R., Singhvi, A., & Yourish, K. (2018, April 24). What happened in the Parkland school shooting. *The New York Times*. Accessed at www.nytimes.com/interactive/2018/02/15/us/florida-school-shooting-map.html on July 12, 2023.

American Association of University Women. (2022). *Where we stand: Title IX*. Accessed at www.aauw.org/resources/policy/position-title-ix on July 12, 2023.

Anderson, J. D. (1988). *The education of Blacks in the South, 1860–1935*. Chapel Hill, NC: University of North Carolina Press.

Assessment. (2015, November 10). In *The glossary of education reform*. Accessed at www.edglossary.org /assessment on July 12, 2023.

Atterbury, A. (2022, May 6). Mystery solved? Florida reveals why it rejected math books over critical race theory. *Politico*. Accessed at www.politico.com/news/2022/05/05/fldoe-releases-math-textbook -reviews-00030503 on July 12, 2023.

Ax, J. (2023, April 19). Florida education board extends ban on gender identity lessons to all grades. *Reuters*. Accessed at www.reuters.com/world/us/florida-education-board-vote-extending-ban-gender -identity-lessons-2023-04-19 on July 12, 2023.

Bailey, J. R., & Rehman, S. (2022, March 4). Don't underestimate the power of self-reflection. *Harvard Business Review*. Accessed at https://hbr.org/2022/03/dont-underestimate-the-power-of-self -reflection on September 25, 2023.

Bailey, K., & Jakicic, C. (2023). *Common formative assessment: A toolkit for Professional Learning Communities at Work* (2nd ed.). Bloomington, IN: Solution Tree Press.

Baker, L. (2022, April 5). Forever changed: A timeline of how COVID upended schools. *Education Week*. Accessed at www.edweek.org/leadership/forever-changed-a-timeline-of-how-covid-upended -schools/2022/04 on July 12, 2023.

Ballis, B., & Heath, K. (2021, May 26). *Special education: Beneficial to many, harmful to others.* Washington, DC: Brookings Institution. Accessed at www.brookings.edu/articles/special-education -beneficial-to-some-harmful-to-others on September 25, 2023.

Barber, M., & Mourshed, M. (2007, September). *How the world's best performing school systems come out on top.* New York: McKinsey & Company. Accessed at www.mckinsey.com/industries/education /our-insights/how-the-worlds-best-performing-school-systems-come-out-on-top on July 12, 2023.

Benchmarks. (2014). *Common Core State Standards adoption map*. Accessed at www .academicbenchmarks.com/ccss-state-status on May 16, 2014.

Bikales, J. (2022, July 30). Okla. downgrades school district over complaint it shamed White people. *The Washington Post*. Accessed at www.washingtonpost.com/education/2022/07/30/crt-oklahoma -tulsa-schools-shame-white on July 12, 2023.

Black, P., & Wiliam, D. (1998). Assessment and classroom learning. *Assessment in Education: Principles, Policy & Practice, 5*(1), 7–75.

Bradberry, T. (2016, September 9). How complaining rewires your brain for negativity. *Entrepreneur*. Accessed at www.entrepreneur.com/growing-a-business/how-complaining-rewires-your-brain-for -negativity/281734 on July 12, 2023.

Braun, H. (2004). Reconsidering the impact of high-stakes testing. *Education Policy Analysis Archives, 12*(1), 1–43.

Brown, B. D., Horn, R. S., & King, G. (2018). The effective implementation of professional learning communities. *Alabama Journal of Educational Leadership, 5*, 53–59.

Brown v. Board of Education, 347 U.S. 483 (1954).

Buffum, A., Mattos, M., & Malone, J. (2018). *Taking action: A handbook for RTI at Work*. Bloomington, IN: Solution Tree Press.

Buffum, A., Mattos, M., & Weber, C. (2010). The why behind RTI. *Educational Leadership, 68*(2). Accessed at www.ascd.org/el/articles/the-why-behind-rti on July 12, 2023.

Buffum, A., Mattos, M., & Weber, C. (2012). *Simplifying response to intervention: Four essential guiding principles*. Bloomington, IN: Solution Tree Press.

Camera, L. (2021, September 7). The looming crisis of kids and COVID. *U.S. News and World Report*. Accessed at www.usnews.com/news/education-news/articles/2021-09-07/schools-approach-critical -juncture-with-kids-and-coronavirus on July 12, 2023.

Card, D., & Rothstein, J. (2006). *Racial segregation and the Black-White test score gap* (Working Paper No. 12078). Cambridge, MA: National Bureau of Economic Research.

Carnegie Corporation of New York. (1989). *Turning points: Preparing American youth for the 21st century*. New York: Author. Accessed at www.carnegie.org/publications/turning-points-preparing -american-youth-for-the-21st-century on July 12, 2023.

Chen, G. (2021, February 17). *A relevant history of public education in the United States* [Blog post]. Accessed at www.publicschoolreview.com/blog/a-relevant-history-of-public-education-in-the -united-states on July 12, 2023.

Cherry, K. (2023, March 12). *B. F. Skinner's life, theories, and influence on psychology*. Accessed at www .verywellmind.com/b-f-skinner-biography-1904-1990-2795543 on July 12, 2023.

Cobb, J. (2021, September 13). The man behind critical race theory. *The New Yorker*. Accessed at www .newyorker.com/magazine/2021/09/20/the-man-behind-critical-race-theory on July 12, 2023.

Coelho, P. (1993). *The alchemist*. New York: HarperCollins.

Coleman, J. S., Campbell, E. Q., Hobson, C. J., McPartland, J., Mood, A. M., Weinfeld, F. D., et al. (1966). *Equality of educational opportunity*. Washington, DC: U.S. Department of Health, Education, and Welfare.

Coleman, M. C. (1985). *Presbyterian missionary attitudes toward American Indians, 1837–1893*. Jackson, MS: University of Mississippi Press.

Collins, J. (2001). *Good to great: Why some companies make the leap . . . and others don't*. New York: Harper Business.

Connell, R. W. (1993). *Schools and social justice*. Philadelphia: Temple University Press.

Conzemius, A. E., & O'Neill, J. (2014). *The handbook for SMART school teams: Revitalizing best practices for collaboration* (2nd ed.). Bloomington, IN: Solution Tree Press.

Couch, M., II, Frost, M., Santiago, J., & Hilton, A. (2021). Rethinking standardized testing from an access, equity and achievement perspective: Has anything changed for African American students? *Journal of Research Initiatives, 5*(3), Article 6.

Cremin, L. A. (Ed.). (1957). *The republic and the school: Horace Mann on the education of free men*. New York: Teachers College Press.

Criterion-referenced test. (2014, April 30). In *The glossary of education reform*. Accessed at www .edglossary.org/criterion-referenced-test on July 12, 2023.

Critical thinking. (2013, August 29). In *The glossary of education reform*. Accessed at www.edglossary .org/critical-thinking on July 12, 2023.

Curriculum. (2015, August 12). In *The glossary of education reform*. Accessed at www.edglossary.org /curriculum on July 12, 2023.

Darcy, A. M. (2023, March 6). The victim mentality: What it is and why you use it. *Harley Therapy Mental Health Blog*. Accessed at www.harleytherapy.co.uk/counselling/victim-mentality.htm on July 12, 2023.

Deal, T. E., & Peterson, K. D. (1999). *Shaping school culture: The heart of leadership*. San Francisco: Jossey-Bass.

Deal, T. E., & Peterson, K. D. (2016). *Shaping school culture* (3rd ed.). San Francisco: Jossey-Bass.

Delgado v. Bastrop Independent School District, Civil Action No. 388 (W.D. Tex. 1948).

Dewey, J. (1939). *Freedom and culture*. New York: Putnam.

Dhuey, E., & Smith, J. (2014). How important are school principals in the production of student achievement? *Canadian Journal of Economics, 47*(2), 634–663.

Dickinson, E. E. (2016, Winter). Coleman Report set the standard for the study of public education. *Johns Hopkins Magazine*. Accessed at https://hub.jhu.edu/magazine/2016/winter/coleman-report -public-education on July 12, 2023.

Doublet, S. (2000). *The stress myth*. Chesterfield, MO: Science and Humanities Press.

Doonan, D., & Kenneally, K. (2022). *Americans' views of public school teachers and personnel in the wake of COVID-19*. Washington, DC: National Institute on Retirement Security.

DuFour, R. (2001). Community: Getting everyone to buy in. *Journal of Staff Development, 22*(4), 3.

DuFour, R. (2004). What is a "professional learning community"? *Educational Leadership, 61*(8). Accessed at www.ascd.org/el/articles/what-is-a-professional-learning-community on July 12, 2023.

DuFour, R. (2007). In praise of top-down leadership. *School Administrator, 64*(10), 38–42.

DuFour, R. (2015). *In praise of American educators: And how they can become even better*. Bloomington, IN: Solution Tree Press.

DuFour, R., & DuFour, R. (2006). The power of professional learning communities. *National Forum of Educational Administration and Supervision Journal, 24*(1), 2–5.

DuFour, R., & DuFour, R. (2012). *The school leader's guide to Professional Learning Communities at Work*. Bloomington, IN: Solution Tree Press.

DuFour, R., DuFour, R., & Eaker, R. (2008). *Revisiting Professional Learning Communities at Work: New insights for improving schools*. Bloomington, IN: Solution Tree Press.

DuFour, R., DuFour, R., Eaker, R., & Many, T. W. (2006). *Learning by doing: A handbook for Professional Learning Communities at Work*. Bloomington, IN: Solution Tree Press.

DuFour, R., DuFour, R., Eaker, R., Many, T. W., & Mattos, M. (2016). *Learning by doing: A handbook for Professional Learning Communities at Work* (3rd ed.). Bloomington, IN: Solution Tree Press.

DuFour, R., DuFour, R., Eaker, R., Mattos, M., & Muhammad, A. (2021). *Revisiting Professional Learning Communities at Work: Proven insights for sustained, substantive school improvement* (2nd ed.). Bloomington, IN: Solution Tree Press.

DuFour, R., DuFour, R., Lopez, D., & Muhammad, A. (2006). Promises kept: Collective commitments to students become a catalyst for improved professional practice. *Journal of Staff Development, 27*(3), 53–56.

DuFour, R., & Eaker, R. (1998). *Professional Learning Communities at Work: Best practices for enhancing student achievement*. Bloomington, IN: Solution Tree Press.

DuFour, R., & Fullan, M. (2013). *Cultures built to last: Systemic PLCs at Work*. Bloomington, IN: Solution Tree Press.

DuFour, R., & Marzano, R. J. (2011). *Leaders of learning: How district, school, and classroom leaders improve student achievement*. Bloomington, IN: Solution Tree Press.

DuFour, R., & Reeves, D. (2016). The futility of PLC Lite. *Phi Delta Kappan, 97*(6), 69–71.

DuFour, R., Reeves, D., & DuFour, R. (2018). *Responding to the Every Student Succeeds Act with the PLC at Work process*. Bloomington, IN: Solution Tree Press.

Dvorsky, G. (2014, March 21). *Why B. F. Skinner may have been the most dangerous psychologist ever*. Accessed at https://gizmodo.com/why-b-f-skinner-may-have-been-the-most-dangerous-psych-1548690441 on July 12, 2023.

Eaker, R. (2020). *A summing up: Teaching and learning in effective schools and PLCs at Work*. Bloomington, IN: Solution Tree Press.

Earl, L. M., & Katz, S. (2006). *Leading schools in a data-rich world: Harnessing data for school improvement*. Thousand Oaks, CA: Corwin Press.

Education Week Staff. (2021, March 4). A year of COVID-19: What it looked like for schools. *Education Week*. Accessed at www.edweek.org/leadership/a-year-of-covid-19-what-it-looked-like-for-schools/2021/03 on September 25, 2023.

Ellerbeck, S. (2023, January 25). *The Great Resignation continues. Why are US workers continuing to quit their jobs?* Accessed at www.weforum.org/agenda/2023/01/us-workers-jobs-quit on July 12, 2023.

Elmore, R. F. (2000, Winter). Building a new structure for school leadership. *American Educator*. Accessed at www.aft.org/sites/default/files/NewStructureWint99_00.pdf on July 12, 2023.

El-Sadr, W. M., Vasan, A., & El-Mohandes, A. (2023). Facing the new COVID-19 reality. *New England Journal of Medicine, 388*(5), 385–387.

Epiphany. (n.d.). In *Merriam-Webster's online dictionary*. Accessed at www.merriam-webster.com /dictionary/epiphany on July 12, 2023.

Erkens, C., Schimmer, T., & Dimich, N. (2018). *Instructional agility: Responding to assessment with real-time decisions*. Bloomington, IN: Solution Tree Press.

Expanded learning time. (2013, August 29). In *The glossary of education reform*. Accessed at www .edglossary.org/expanded-learning-time on July 12, 2023.

Faircloth, S. C. (2020, Winter). The education of American Indian students. *American Educator*. Accessed at www.aft.org/ae/winter2020-2021/faircloth_sb1 on September 25, 2023.

Fix, R. L. (2021). Pernicious executive order 13950 revoked, yet structural racism looms large. *Leadership, 17*(6), 747–751.

Fortin, J. (2022, July 18). More pandemic fallout: The chronically absent student. *The New York Times*. Accessed at www.nytimes.com/2022/04/20/us/school-absence-attendance-rate-covid.html on July 12, 2023.

Frick, M. (2020, November 22). CDC removes guidelines encouraging in-person learning amid COVID-19 pandemic. *MLive*. Accessed at www.mlive.com/news/2020/11/cdc-removes-guidelines -encouraging-in-person-learning-amid-covid-19-pandemic.html on July 12, 2023.

Friziellie, H., Schmidt, J. A., & Spiller, J. (2016). *Yes we can! General and special educators collaborating in a professional learning community*. Bloomington, IN: Solution Tree Press.

Gewertz, C. (2014, February 19). Poll: Building character more important goal of K–12 ed. than building economy. *Education Week*. Accessed at www.edweek.org/leadership/poll-building -character-more-important-goal-of-k-12-ed-than-building-economy/2014/02 on July 12, 2023.

Glaser, J. E. (2013, February 28). Your brain is hooked on being right. *Harvard Business Review*. Accessed at https://hbr.org/2013/02/break-your-addiction-to-being on July 12, 2023.

Goldhaber, D., & Holden, K. (2020). *Understanding the early teacher pipeline: What we can (and, importantly, can't) learn from national data* (Policy Brief No. 21-1120). Washington, DC: National Center for Analysis of Longitudinal Data in Educational Research.

Goldhaber, D., Kane, T. J., McEachin, A., Morton, E., Patterson, T., & Staiger, D. O. (2022). *The consequences of remote and hybrid instruction during the pandemic* (Working Paper No. 30010). Cambridge, MA: Center for Education Policy Research, Harvard University.

Gonzalez, G. G. (1990). *Chicano education in the era of segregation*. Philadelphia: Balch Institute Press.

Gonzales, M. G. (2019). *Mexicanos: A history of Mexicans in the United States* (3rd ed.). Bloomington, IN: Indiana University Press.

Gotlib, I. H., Miller, J. G., Borchers, L. R., Coury, S. M., Costello, L. A., Garcia, J. M., et al. (2022). Effects of COVID-19 pandemic on mental health and brain maturation in adolescents: Implications for analyzing longitudinal data. *Biological Psychology: Global Open Science*. Accessed at www.bpsgos .org/action/showPdf?pii=S2667-1743%2822%2900142-2 on July 12, 2023.

Groves, H. E. (1951). Separate but equal: The doctrine of *Plessy vs. Ferguson. Phylon, 12*(1), 66–72.

Gruenert, S., & Whitaker, T. (2015). *School culture rewired: How to define, assess, and transform it*. Alexandria, VA: ASCD.

Guardino, P. (2017). *The dead march: A history of the Mexican-American War*. Cambridge, MA: Harvard University Press.

Guskey, T. R. (2015). *On your mark: Challenging the conventions of grading and reporting*. Bloomington, IN: Solution Tree Press.

Guskey, T. R. (2017, June 1). Why do we recycle and sometimes misuse educational words? *Education Week*. Accessed at www.edweek.org/education/opinion-why-do-we-recycle-and-sometimes-misuse -educational-words/2017/06 on July 12, 2023.

Haberman, M., & Brubaker, D. L. (1970). The art of schoolsmanship. *Journal of Teacher Education*, *21*(3), 451–452.

Hall, B. (2022). *Powerful guiding coalitions: How to build and sustain the leadership team in your PLC at Work*. Bloomington, IN: Solution Tree Press.

Halloran, C., Jack, R., Okun, J. C., & Oster, E. (2021). *Pandemic schooling mode and student test scores: Evidence from US states* (Working Paper No. 29497). Cambridge, MA: National Bureau of Economic Research.

Hamilton, L. S., Stecher, B. M., & Yuan, K. (2008). *Standards-based reform in the United States: History, research, and future directions*. Washington, DC: Center on Education Policy.

Hammond, Z. (2015). *Culturally responsive teaching and the brain: Promoting authentic engagement and rigor among culturally and linguistically diverse students*. Thousand Oaks, CA: Corwin Press.

Hansen, A. (2015). *How to develop PLCs for singletons and small schools*. Bloomington, IN: Solution Tree Press.

Harrell, G. (2022, July 28). Veterans can now teach in Florida with no degree. School leaders say it "lowers the bar." *The Gainesville Sun*. Accessed at www.gainesville.com/story/news/2022/07/20 /military-veterans-spouses-can-now-teach-without-degree-florida/10084909002 on July 12, 2023.

Hattie, J. A. C. (2009). *Visible learning: A synthesis of over 800 meta-analyses relating to achievement*. New York: Routledge.

Hattie, J. A. C. (2020, April 14). *Visible learning effect sizes when schools are closed: What matters and what does not*. Accessed at https://corwin-connect.com/2020/04/visible-learning-effect-sizes-when-schools-are-closed-what-matters-and-what-does-not/#.XrWiW1mhkO0.email on July 12, 2023.

Hess, F. M. (2011, Fall). Our achievement-gap mania. *National Affairs*, *9*, 113–129.

Heubeck, E. (2023, April 26). Two-thirds of teachers say schools are falling short for struggling learners. *Education Week*. Accessed at www.edweek.org/teaching-learning/two-thirds-of-teachers -say-schools-are-falling-short-for-struggling-learners/2023/04 on July 12, 2023.

Hinds, H., Newby, L. D. T., & Korman, H. T. N. (2022, September). *Ignored, punished, and underserved: Understanding and addressing disparities in education experiences and outcomes for Black children with disabilities*. Washington, DC: Bellwether. Accessed at https://bellwether.org/wp -content/uploads/2022/09/IgnoredPunishedandUnderserved_Bellwether_September2022.pdf on July 12, 2023.

Hoffer, E. (1951). *The true believer: Thoughts on the nature of mass movements*. New York: Harper & Row.

Holcomb, E. L. (2012). *Data dynamics: Aligning teacher team, school, and district efforts*. Bloomington, IN: Solution Tree Press.

Honders, C. (2017). *Mexican American civil rights movement*. New York: PowerKids Press.

Hord, S. M. (1997). Professional learning communities: What are they and why are they important? *Issues . . . about Change*, *6*(1). Accessed at https://sedl.org/change/issues/issues61.html on July 12, 2023.

Hudson, C. G. (2005). Socioeconomic status and mental illness: Tests of the social causation and selection hypotheses. *American Journal of Orthopsychiatry*, *75*(1), 3–18.

Jackson, A. W., & Davis, G. A. (2000). *Turning points 2000: Educating adolescents in the 21st century*. New York: Teachers College Press.

Jackson, Y. (2011). *The pedagogy of confidence: Inspiring high intellectual performance in urban schools*. New York: Teachers College Press.

Jacobson, L. (2019, April 8). *AERA '19: Testing policies are the "Jim Crow of education," association president suggests*. Accessed at www.k12dive.com/news/aera-19-testing-policies-are-the-jim-crow-of -education-association-pre/552188 on July 12, 2023.

Jain, A., Bodicherla, K. P., Raza, Q., & Sahu, K. K. (2020). Impact on mental health by "living in isolation and quarantine" during COVID-19 pandemic. *Journal of Family Medicine and Primary Care, 9*(10), 5415–5418.

Jensen, E. (2016). *Poor students, rich teaching: Mindsets for change.* Bloomington, IN: Solution Tree Press.

Jensen, E. (2019). *Poor students, rich teaching: Seven high-impact mindsets for students from poverty* (Rev. ed.). Bloomington, IN: Solution Tree Press.

Jones, J. (2004). *Soldiers of light and love: Northern teachers and Georgia Blacks, 1865–1873.* Athens, GA: University of Georgia Press.

Jones, N. D., Camburn, E. M., Kelcey, B., & Quintero, E. (2022). Teachers' time use and affect before and after COVID-19 school closures. *AERA Open, 8*(1), 1–14.

Joyce, K. (2022, July 12). We don't need no education: Now Arizona says teachers don't require college degrees. *Salon.* Accessed at www.salon.com/2022/07/12/we-dont-need-no-education-now-arizona-says-teachers-dont-require-college-degrees on July 12, 2023.

Kaestle, C. F. (1983). *Pillars of the republic: Common schools and American society, 1780–1860.* New York: Hill and Wang.

Kanold, T. D. (2011). *The five disciplines of PLC leaders.* Bloomington, IN: Solution Tree Press.

Kanold, T. D. (2021). *SOUL! Fulfilling the promise of your professional life as a teacher and leader.* Bloomington, IN: Solution Tree Press.

Katzenmeyer, M., & Moller, G. (2009). *Awakening the sleeping giant: Helping teachers develop as leaders* (3rd ed.). Thousand Oaks, CA: Corwin Press.

Kennedy, M. (2005). *Inside teaching: How classroom life undermines reform.* Cambridge, MA: Harvard University Press.

Key, J., & Eaker, R. (2023, May 7). Does Arkansas—the land of opportunity—have the solution to America's public education crisis? [Advertisement]. *The New York Times.*

Klein, A. (2010, February 9). Debate heats up over replacing AYP metric in ESEA. *Education Week.* Accessed at www.edweek.org/policy-politics/debate-heats-up-over-replacing-ayp-metric-in-esea/2010/02/00000175-edbc-de5b-a77d-ffbe75250000 on July 12, 2023.

Kliewer, A., Mahmud, M., & Wayland, B. (2023). "Kill the Indian, save the man": Remembering the stories of Indian boarding schools. *Gaylord News.* Accessed at www.ou.edu/gaylord/exiled-to-indian-country/content/remembering-the-stories-of-indian-boarding-schools on September 25, 2023.

Kotter, J. P. (2012). *Leading change.* Cambridge, MA: Harvard Business Review Press.

Koumpilova, M. (2022, February 23). *In Chicago Public Schools, more principals and teachers are leaving.* Accessed at https://chicago.chalkbeat.org/2022/2/23/22947818/chicago-public-schools-teacher-principal-resignation-retirement-covid on July 12, 2023.

Kozol, J. (1991). *Savage inequalities: Children in America's schools.* New York: Crown.

Kurland, N. B., & Pelled, L. H. (2000). Passing the word: Toward a model of gossip and power in the workplace. *Academy of Management Review, 25*(2), 428–438.

Ladson-Billings, G., & Tate, W. F. (1995). Toward a critical race theory of education. *Teachers College Record, 97*(1), 47–68.

Lawrence, D. F., Loi, N. M., & Gudex, B. W. (2019). Understanding the relationship between work intensification and burnout in secondary teachers. *Teachers and Teaching, 25*(2), 189–199.

Leane, B., & Yost, J. (2022). *Singletons in a PLC at Work: Navigating on-ramps to meaningful collaboration.* Bloomington, IN: Solution Tree Press.

Learning gap. (2013, August 29). In *The glossary of education reform.* Accessed at www.edglossary.org/learning-gap on July 12, 2023.

Learning standards. (2014, February 4). In *The glossary of education reform*. Accessed at www.edglossary .org/learning-standards on July 12, 2023.

Lehrer-Small, A. (2021, June 9). *One fate, two fates, red states, blue states: New data reveal a 432-hour in-person learning gap produced by the politics of pandemic schooling*. Accessed at www.the74million .org/article/one-fate-two-fates-red-states-blue-states-new-data-reveals-a-432-hour-in-person -learning-gap-produced-by-the-politics-of-pandemic-schooling on July 12, 2023.

Lencioni, P. (2002). *The five dysfunctions of a team: A leadership fable*. San Francisco: Jossey-Bass.

Lencioni, P. (2012). *The advantage: Why organizational health trumps everything else in business*. San Francisco: Jossey-Bass.

Lenzen, C. (2022, December 27). *"When retail is somehow less stressful than education": Former teacher now works for Costco, says "everything is better."* Accessed at www.dailydot.com/irl/former-teacher -works-at-costco on July 12, 2023.

Lillard, P. P. (2011). *Montessori: A modern approach*. New York: Schocken Books.

Little, J. W., & McLaughlin, M. W. (Eds.). (1993). *Teachers' work: Individuals, colleagues, and contexts*. New York: Teachers College Press.

Lopez, N. (2003). *Hopeful girls, troubled boys: Race and gender disparity in urban education*. New York: Routledge.

Lortie, D. C. (1975). *Schoolteacher: A sociological study*. Chicago: University of Chicago Press.

Loveless, T. (2013). *The 2013 Brown Center Report on American education: How well are American students learning?* Washington, DC: Brookings Institution.

Lynchpin. (n.d.). In *Merriam-Webster's online dictionary*. Accessed at www.merriam-webster.com /dictionary/lynchpin on July 12, 2023.

Manna, P. (2006). *School's in: Federalism and the national education agenda*. Washington, DC: Georgetown University Press.

Many, T. W. (2006). Matching classroom instruction with common assessments. *TEPSA Journal, Summer*, 6–8.

Marianno, B. D., Hemphill, A. A., Loures-Elias, A. P. S., Garcia, L., Cooper, D., & Coombes, E. (2022). Power in a pandemic: Teachers' unions and their responses to school reopening. *AERA Open, 8*(1), 1–16.

Martin, W. E., Jr. (Ed.). (2020). *Brown v. Board of Education: A brief history with documents* (2nd ed.). Boston: Bedford/St. Martin's.

Marzano, R. J. (2003). *What works in schools: Translating research into action*. Alexandria, VA: ASCD.

Marzano, R. J. (2009a). *Getting serious about school reform: Three critical commitments*. Marzano & Associates.

Marzano, R. J. (2009b). Setting the record straight on "high-yield" strategies. *Phi Delta Kappan, 91*(1), 30–37.

Marzano, R. J., Warrick, P. B., & Simms, J. A. (2014). *A handbook for High Reliability Schools: The next step in school reform*. Bloomington, IN: Marzano Resources.

Marzano, R. J., & Waters, T. (2009). *District leadership that works: Striking the right balance*. Bloomington, IN: Solution Tree Press.

Masur, L. P. (2011). *The Civil War: A concise history*. New York: Oxford University Press.

Mattos, M., DuFour, R., DuFour, R., Eaker, R., & Many, T. W. (2016). *Concise answers to frequently asked questions about Professional Learning Communities at Work*. Bloomington, IN: Solution Tree Press.

McCarthy, C. J., Blaydes, M., Weppner, C. H., & Lambert, R. G. (2022). Teacher stress and COVID-19: Where do we go from here? *Phi Delta Kappan, 104*(1), 12–17. Accessed at https://kappanonline .org/teacher-stress-covid-19-mccarthy-blaydes-weppner-lambert on July 12, 2023.

McGregor, D. (1960). *The human side of enterprise*. New York: McGraw-Hill.

McLaughlin, M. W., & Talbert, J. E. (2006). *Building school-based teacher learning communities: Professional strategies to improve student achievement*. New York: Teachers College Press.

Meckler, L., & Natanson, H. (2022, February 14). Critical race theory laws have teachers scared, confused and self-censoring. *The Washington Post*. Accessed at www.washingtonpost.com /education/2022/02/14/critical-race-theory-teachers-fear-laws on July 12, 2023.

Melago, C. (2008, February 3). Left in the dark over No Child Left Behind. *New York Daily News*.

Melnick, R. S. (2018). *The transformation of Title IX: Regulating gender equality in education*. Washington, DC: Brookings Institution Press.

Mendez v. Westminster School District of Orange County, et al., 64 F. Supp. 544 (S.D. Cal. 1946).

Muhammad, A. (2009). *Transforming school culture: How to overcome staff division*. Bloomington, IN: Solution Tree Press.

Muhammad, A. (2015). *Overcoming the achievement gap trap: Liberating mindsets to effect change*. Bloomington, IN: Solution Tree Press.

Muhammad, A. (2018). *Transforming school culture: How to overcome staff division* (2nd ed.). Bloomington, IN: Solution Tree Press.

Muhammad, A., & Cruz, L. F. (2019). *Time for change: Four essential skills for transformational school and district leaders*. Bloomington, IN: Solution Tree Press.

Muhammad, A., & Hollie, S. (2012). *The will to lead, the skill to teach: Transforming schools at every level*. Bloomington, IN: Solution Tree Press.

Natanson, H., & Meckler, L. (2020, November 27). Remote school is leaving children sad and angry. *The Washington Post*. Accessed at www.washingtonpost.com/education/2020/11/27/remote-learning -emotional-toll on July 12, 2023.

National Education Association. (2022). *What you need to know about Florida's "Don't Say Gay or Trans" bill*. Accessed at www.nea.org/sites/default/files/2022-04/What%20You%20Need%20to%20Know _revise.pdf on July 12, 2023.

Nelson, S. (2023). *Education in the new world, 1630–1776*. Accessed at https://newworldeducation .weebly.com/new-england-colonies.html on February 20, 2023.

No Child Left Behind (NCLB) Act of 2001, Pub. L. No. 107-110, § 115, Stat. 1425 (2002).

Orfield, G. (2001, July). *Schools more separate: Consequences of a decade of resegregation*. Cambridge, MA: Civil Rights Project, Harvard University.

O'Shea, M. R. (2005). *From standards to success: A guide for school leaders*. Alexandria, VA: ASCD.

Panchal, N., Saunders, H., & Rudowitz, R. (2023, March 20). *The implications of COVID-19 for mental health and substance use*. Accessed at www.kff.org/coronavirus-covid-19/issue-brief/the-implications -of-covid-19-for-mental-health-and-substance-use on July 12, 2023.

Paradigm shift. (n.d.). In *Merriam-Webster's online dictionary*. Accessed at www.merriam-webster.com /dictionary/paradigm%20shift on July 12, 2023.

Personalized learning. (2015, May 14). In *The glossary of education reform*. Accessed at www.edglossary .org/personalized-learning on July 12, 2023.

Peterson, J., & Densley, J. (2021). *The violence project: How to stop a mass shooting epidemic*. New York: Abrams Press.

Peterson, P. E., & Hess, F. (2008). Few states set world-class standards: In fact, most render the notion of proficiency meaningless. *Education Next, 8*(3). Accessed at www.educationnext.org/few-states-set -worldclass-standards on July 12, 2023.

Petrides, L., & Nodine, T. (2005). *Anatomy of school system improvement: Performance-driven practices in urban school districts*. Half Moon Bay, CA: Institute for the Study of Knowledge Management in Education.

Pfeffer, J., & Sutton, R. I. (2000). *The knowing-doing gap: How smart companies turn knowledge into action*. Boston: Harvard Business School Press.

Pink, D. H. (2011). *Drive: The surprising truth about what motivates us*. New York: Riverhead Books.

Pitofsky, M. (2023, February 10). Florida rejected AP African American Studies. Here's what's actually being taught in the course. *USA Today*. Accessed at www.usatoday.com/story/news/education/2023/02/01/florida-ap-african-american-studies-framework/11136117002 on July 12, 2023.

Plessy v. Ferguson, 163 U.S. 537 (1896).

Pole, J. R. (1993). *The pursuit of equality in American history* (Rev. ed.). Berkeley, CA: University of California Press.

Polikoff, M. (2021). *Beyond standards: The fragmentation of education governance and the promise of curriculum reform*. Cambridge, MA: Harvard Education Press.

Popham, W. J. (2006, April 18). Educator cheating on No Child Left Behind tests. *Education Week*. Accessed at www.edweek.org/teaching-learning/opinion-educator-cheating-on-no-child-left-behind-tests/2006/04 on July 12, 2023.

Popham, W. J. (2013, January 8). Waving the flag for formative assessment. *Education Week*. Accessed at www.edweek.org/teaching-learning/opinion-waving-the-flag-for-formative-assessment/2013/01 on July 12, 2023.

Popham, W. J. (2021, December 1). The misuse of testing: Standardized tests should help, not harm students. *American School Board Journal*. Accessed at www.nsba.org/ASBJ/2021/december/the-misuse-of-testing on July 12, 2023.

Prucha, F. P. (Ed.). (1990). *Documents of United States Indian policy* (2nd ed.). Lincoln, NE: University of Nebraska Press.

Rademacher, T. (2017, November 21). *Why the phrase "with fidelity" is an affront to good teaching*. Accessed at www.chalkbeat.org/2017/11/21/21103830/why-the-phrase-with-fidelity-is-an-affront-to-good-teaching on July 12, 2023.

Ramirez, M. (2022, August 27). For many students across the U.S., segregated schools are still a reality. Here's why. *USA Today*. Accessed at www.usatoday.com/story/news/2022/08/27/school-segregation-affects-more-than-third-u-s-students/10342799002 on October 2, 2023.

Rasmussen Reports. (2010, May 11). *73% say being a teacher is one of the most important jobs*. Accessed at www.rasmussenreports.com/public_content/lifestyle/general_lifestyle/may_2010/73_say_being_a_teacher_is_one_of_the_most_important_jobs on December 4, 2010.

Reeves, D. (2021). *Deep change leadership: A model for renewing and strengthening schools and districts*. Bloomington, IN: Solution Tree Press.

Reeves, D., & Eaker, R. (2019). *100-day leaders: Turning short-term wins into long-term success in schools*. Bloomington, IN: Solution Tree Press.

Relevance. (2013, August 29). In *The glossary of education reform*. Accessed at www.edglossary.org/relevance on July 12, 2023.

Reyhner, J. (2018). American Indian boarding schools: What went wrong? What is going right? *Journal of American Indian Education*, *57*(1), 58–78.

Riddell, R., & Arundel, K. (2022, July 22). *Florida to let veterans teach without bachelor's degree*. Accessed at www.k12dive.com/news/florida-to-let-veterans-spouses-teach-without-bachelors-degree/627965 on July 12, 2023.

Riegel, D. G. (2018, October 12). Stop complaining about your colleagues behind their backs. *Harvard Business Review*. Accessed at https://hbr.org/2018/10/stop-complaining-about-your-colleagues-behind-their-backs on July 12, 2023.

Rigor. (2014, December 29). In *The glossary of education reform*. Accessed at www.edglossary.org/rigor on July 12, 2023.

Riser-Kositsky, M. (2021, November 22). Education statistics: Facts about American schools. *Education Week*. Accessed at www.edweek.org/leadership/education-statistics-facts-about-american-schools /2019/01 on July 12, 2023.

Rist, R. C. (Ed.). (1979). *Desegregated schools: Appraisals of an American experiment*. New York: Academic Press.

Rogers, K. (2021, June 28). *Life after the 1918 flu has lessons for our post-pandemic world*. Accessed at www.cnn.com/2021/06/28/health/changes-after-covid-pandemic-1918-flu-wellness-scn/index.html on July 12, 2023.

Ryan, B. (2023). *The brilliance in the building: Effecting change in urban schools with the PLC at Work process*. Bloomington, IN: Solution Tree Press.

Ryan, R. M., & Deci, E. L. (2000). Self-determination theory and the facilitation of intrinsic motivation, social development, and well-being. *American Psychologist, 55*(1), 68–78.

Safarpour, A., Lazer, D., Lin, J., Pippert, C. H., Druckman, J., Baum, M., et al. (2021, December). *The COVID States Project #73: American attitudes toward critical race theory*. Accessed at https://osf.io /crv95 on July 12, 2023.

Sahlberg, P. (2021). *Finnish lessons 3.0: What can the world learn from educational change in Finland?* (3rd ed.). New York: Teachers College Press.

Samuels, C. A. (2019, January 8). Special education is broken. *Education Week*. Accessed at www .edweek.org/teaching-learning/special-education-is-broken/2019/01 on July 12, 2023.

San Miguel, G., Jr. (1987). *"Let all of them take heed": Mexican Americans and the campaign for educational equality in Texas, 1910–1981*. Austin, TX: University of Texas Press.

Sawchuk, S. (2021, May 18). What is critical race theory and why is it under attack? *Education Week*. Accessed at www.edweek.org/leadership/what-is-critical-race-theory-and-why-is-it-under-attack /2021/05 on July 12, 2023.

Schement, J. R. (2001). Imagining fairness: Equality and equity of access in search of democracy. In N. Kranich (Ed.), *Libraries and democracy: The cornerstones of liberty* (pp. 15–27). Chicago: American Library Association.

Schimmer, T. (2023). *Redefining student accountability: A proactive approach to teaching behavior outside the gradebook*. Bloomington, IN: Solution Tree Press.

Schmoker, M. (2006). *Results now: How we can achieve unprecedented improvements in teaching and learning*. Alexandria, VA: ASCD.

Schwartz, S. (2021a, March 31). "You can't follow CDC guidelines": What schools really look like during COVID-19. *Education Week*. Accessed at www.edweek.org/leadership/you-cant-follow-cdc -guidelines-what-schools-really-look-like-during-covid-19/2021/03 on July 12, 2023.

Schwartz, S. (2021b, June 11). Map: Where critical race theory is under attack. *Education Week*. Accessed at www.edweek.org/policy-politics/map-where-critical-race-theory-is-under-attack/2021 /06 on July 12, 2023.

Schwartz, S. (2022a, November 28). The architects of the standards movement say they missed a big piece. *Education Week*. Accessed at www.edweek.org/teaching-learning/the-architects-of-the -standards-movement-say-they-missed-a-big-piece/2022/11 on July 12, 2023.

Schwartz, S. (2022b, November 30). COVID hurt student learning: Key findings from a year of research. *Education Week*. Accessed at www.edweek.org/leadership/covid-hurt-student-learning-key -findings-from-a-year-of-research/2022/11 on July 12, 2023.

Senge, P. M. (1990). *The fifth discipline: The art and practice of the learning organization*. New York: Doubleday/Currency.

Senge, P. M. (2006). *The fifth discipline: The art and practice of the learning organization* (Rev. ed.). New York: Doubleday/Currency.

Sergiovanni, T. J. (1993, April 13). *Organizations or communities? Changing the metaphor changes the theory* [Conference presentation]. Annual meeting of the American Educational Research Association, Atlanta, GA.

Sergiovanni, T. J. (1994). Organizations or communities? Changing the metaphor changes the theory. *Educational Administration Quarterly, 30*(2), 214–226.

Shapin, S. (2022). Hard science, soft science: A political history of a disciplinary array. *History of Science, 60*(3), 287–328.

Sinek, S. (2017). *Find your why: A practical guide for discovering purpose for you or your team.* New York: Portfolio/Penguin.

Singer, D. G., & Revenson, T. A. (1978). *A Piaget primer: How a child thinks.* New York: International Universities Press.

Sparks, D. (1999). Assessment without victims: An interview with Rick Stiggins. *Journal of Staff Development, 20*(2), 54–56.

Sparks, S. D. (2022a, July 7). Teacher and student absenteeism is getting worse. *Education Week.* Accessed at www.edweek.org/leadership/teacher-and-student-absenteeism-is-getting-worse/2022/07 on July 12, 2023.

Sparks, S. D. (2022b, December 2). Teen brains aged prematurely during the pandemic. Schools should take note. *Education Week.* Accessed at www.edweek.org/leadership/teen-brains-aged-prematurely -during-the-pandemic-schools-should-take-note/2022/12 on July 12, 2023.

Spiggle, T. (2021, February 3). Why Biden's repeal of the anti-bias training ban was so important for federal employees. *Forbes.* Accessed at www.forbes.com/sites/tomspiggle/2021/02/03/why-bidens -repeal-of-the-anti-bias-training-ban-was-so-important-for-federal-employees/?sh=6d5a46dd525b on July 12, 2023.

Spring, J. (2022). *American education* (20th ed.). New York: Routledge.

Springer, K. (2010). *Educational research: A contextual approach.* Hoboken, NJ: Wiley.

Steele, C. M. (1997). A threat in the air: How stereotypes shape intellectual identity and performance. *American Psychologist, 52*(6), 613–629.

Stiggins, R. (2002). Assessment crisis: The absence of assessment for learning. *Phi Delta Kappan, 83*(10), 758–765.

Sullivan, A. L., & Bal, A. (2013). Disproportionality in special education: Effects of individual and school variables on disability risk. *Exceptional Children, 79*(4), 475–495.

Summative assessment. (2013, August 29). In *The glossary of education reform.* Accessed at www .edglossary.org/summative-assessment on July 12, 2023.

Superville, D. R. (2023, April 20). Why teachers are turning down lucrative offers to stay at this Texas school. *Education Week.* Accessed at www.edweek.org/leadership/why-teachers-are-turning-down -lucrative-offers-to-stay-at-this-texas-school/2023/04 on July 12, 2023.

Suran, S., Pattanaik, V., & Draheim, D. (2020). Frameworks for collective intelligence: A systematic literature review. *ACM Computing Surveys, 53*(1), 1–36.

Sutcher, L., Darling-Hammond, L., & Carver-Thomas, D. (2016). *A coming crisis in teaching? Teacher supply, demand, and shortages in the U.S.* Palo Alto, CA: Learning Policy Institute.

Szasz, M. (1974). *Education and the American Indian: The road to self-determination, 1928–1973.* Albuquerque, NM: University of New Mexico Press.

Team. (n.d.). In *Merriam-Webster's online dictionary.* Accessed at www.merriam-webster.com/dictionary /team on July 12, 2023.

Thernstrom, A., & Thernstrom, S. (2003). *No excuses: Closing the racial gap in learning.* New York: Simon & Schuster.

Tichy, N. M. (1997). *The leadership engine: How winning companies build leaders at every level*. New York: Harper Business.

Turnbull, H. R., III, Stowe, M. J., & Huerta, N. E. (2007). *Free appropriate public education: The law and children with disabilities* (7th ed.). Denver, CO: Love.

Tyack, D., & Cuban, L. (1995). *Tinkering toward utopia: A century of public school reform*. Cambridge, MA: Harvard University Press.

Urbina, I. (2010, January 11). As school exit tests prove tough, states ease standards. *The New York Times*. Accessed at www.nytimes.com/2010/01/12/education/12exit.html on July 12, 2023.

U.S. Department of Education. (2017). *Individuals With Disabilities Education Act: Sec. 300.1 (a)*. Accessed at https://sites.ed.gov/idea/regs/b/a/300.1/a on October 2, 2023.

U.S. Department of Education. (2022, December). *Frequently asked questions: Elementary and Secondary School Emergency Relief Programs, Governor's Emergency Relief Programs*. Washington, DC: Author. Accessed at https://oese.ed.gov/files/2022/12/ESSER-and-GEER-Use-of-Funds-FAQs-December-7-2022-Update-1.pdf on July 12, 2023.

Viadero, D. (2006, July 25). Test scores linked to home prices. *Education Week*. Accessed at www.edweek.org/education/test-scores-linked-to-home-prices/2006/07 on July 12, 2023.

Viadero, D. (2010, February 5). Study finds wide achievement gaps for top students. *Education Week*. Accessed at www.edweek.org/leadership/study-finds-wide-achievement-gaps-for-top-students/2010/02 on July 12, 2023.

Vodicka, D. (2020). *Learner-centered leadership: A blueprint for transformational change in learning communities*. San Diego, CA: IMpress.

Wagner, L., & Dejka, J. (2022, May 9). How are Nebraska school districts spending federal COVID relief? *Omaha World-Herald*. Accessed at https://omaha.com/news/local/education/how-are-nebraska-school-districts-spending-federal-covid-relief/article_d2fd44aa-ccee-11ec-85c7-afa616593d19.html on July 12, 2023.

Walker, T. D. (2016, September 29). The ticking clock of teacher burnout. *The Atlantic*. Accessed at www.theatlantic.com/education/archive/2016/09/the-ticking-clock-of-us-teacher-burnout/502253 on July 12, 2023.

Waxman, O. B. (2022, June 30). Anti-"critical race theory" laws are working. Teachers are thinking twice about how they talk about race. *Time*. Accessed at https://time.com/6192708/critical-race-theory-teachers-racism on July 12, 2023.

Weber, L. (2021, December 14). Bozeman School Board passes controversial equity policy with the word "equity" removed. *Bozeman Daily Chronicle*. Accessed at www.bozemandailychronicle.com/news/education/bozeman-school-board-passes-controversial-equity-policy-with-the-word-equity-removed/article_220be97e-f697-5d62-a2a9-b8a9dd0b24f0.html on July 12, 2023.

Weber, M. (2019). *Economy and society: A new translation* (K. Tribe, Ed. & Trans.). Cambridge, MA: Harvard University Press.

Weichel, M., McCann, B., & Williams, T. (2018). *When they already know it: How to extend and personalize student learning in a PLC at Work*. Bloomington, IN: Solution Tree Press.

Wiliam, D., & Thompson, M. (2008). Integrating assessment with learning: What will it take to make it work? In C. A. Dwyer (Ed.), *The future of assessment: Shaping teaching and learning* (pp. 53–82). Mahwah, NJ: Erlbaum.

Will, M. (2022a, April 14). Teacher job satisfaction hits an all-time low. *Education Week*. Accessed at www.edweek.org/teaching-learning/teacher-job-satisfaction-hits-an-all-time-low/2022/04 on July 12, 2023.

Will, M. (2022b, September 6). How bad is the teacher shortage? What two new studies say. *Education Week*. Accessed at www.edweek.org/leadership/how-bad-is-the-teacher-shortage-what-two-new-studies-say/2022/09 on July 12, 2023.

Williams, K. C., & Hierck, T. (2015). *Starting a movement: Building culture from the inside out in professional learning communities*. Bloomington, IN: Solution Tree Press.

Willis, W. B. (1998). *The Adinkra dictionary: A visual primer of the language of Adinkra*. Ann Arbor, MI: Pyramid Complex.

Wilson, B., & Stamp, E. (2022, November 26). *Hartford sees highest homicide rates in decades*. WTNH. Accessed at www.wtnh.com/news/connecticut/hartford/hartfords-homicide-rate-reaches-highest -number-in-decades on September 25, 2023.

Winerip, M. (2007, December 9). In gaps at school, weighing family life. *The New York Times*. Accessed at www.nytimes.com/2007/12/09/nyregion/nyregionspecial2/09Rparenting.html on July 12, 2023.

Winzer, M. A. (1993). *The history of special education: From isolation to integration*. Washington, DC: Gallaudet University Press.

Wittrock, Q. R. (2023, February 28). *The broke woke joke*. Accessed at https://principlebasedpolitics.org /the-broke-woke-joke on July 12, 2023.

Woolley, A. W., Chabris, C. F., Pentland, A., Hashmi, N., & Malone, T. W. (2010). Evidence for a collective intelligence factor in performance of human groups. *Science*, *330*(6004), 686–688.

Yell, M. L., Rogers, D., & Rogers, E. L. (1998). The legal history of special education: What a long, strange trip it's been! *Remedial and Special Education*, *19*(4), 219–228.

YouthTruth Student Survey. (2022). *Insights from the student experience, part I: Emotional and mental health*. San Francisco: Author. Accessed at https://youthtruthsurvey.org/wp-content/uploads/2023 /07/EMH_2022.pdf on July 12, 2023.

Zirkel, P. A., & Kincaid, J. M. (1995). *Section 504, the ADA and the schools*. Horsham, PA: LRP.

Index

Beyond Conversations About Race
Washington Collado, Sharroky Hollie, Rosa Isiah, Yvette Jackson, Anthony Muhammad, Douglas Reeves, and Kenneth C. Williams

Written by a collective of brilliant authors, this essential work provokes respectful dialogue about race that catalyzes school-changing action. Learn how to talk about race in the classroom and discover actionable steps you can take toward promoting a safe, equitable environment for marginalized students and underserved communities.

BKG035

Transforming School Culture
Anthony Muhammad

This *Second Edition* provides a school improvement plan for leaders to overcome staff division, improve relationships, and build positive school cultures. Learn school leadership techniques for addressing the four types of teachers that impact your school culture.

BKF793

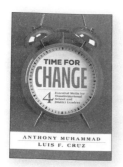

Time for Change
Anthony Muhammad and Luis F. Cruz

Discover how to develop and strengthen the four essential skills of effective educational leaders. Inspire a shared vision of strategic change and overcome resistance through strong communication, trust building, empowerment of those you lead, and a focus on results.

BKF683

Overcoming the Achievement Gap Trap
Anthony Muhammad

Explore strategies for adopting a new mindset that frees educators and students from negative academic performance expectations.

BKF618